D0883085

# By His Own Hand?

# BY HIS OWN HAND?

# The Mysterious Death of Meriwether Lewis

*Edited by John D. W. Guice*

*Contributions by James J. Holmberg,*
*John D. W. Guice, and Jay H. Buckley*

Introduction by Clay S. Jenkinson

Foreword by Elliott West

Oklahoma University Press : Norman

**ALSO BY JOHN D. W. GUICE**

*The Rocky Mountain Bench: The Territorial Supreme Courts of Colorado, Montana, and Wyoming, 1861–1890* (New Haven, 1972)
(introduction to facsimile ed.) *Life and Confession of the Noted Outlaw, James Copeland,* by J. R. S. Pitts (Jackson, Miss., 1980)
(with Thomas D. Clark) *The Old Southwest, 1795–1830: Frontiers in Conflict* (Albuquerque, 1989; Norman, 1996)
*Forrest County General Hospital, 1952–2002: The Evolution of a Regional Referral Center: A Prophecy Fulfilled* (Jackson, Miss., 2002)

**LIBRARY OF CONGRESS CATALOGING-IN-PUBLICATION DATA**
Guice, John D. W.
By his own hand? : the mysterious death of Meriwether Lewis / by John D. W. Guice, James J. Holmberg, and Jay H. Buckley ; introduction by Clay S. Jenkinson ; foreword by Elliott West.
p. cm.
Includes bibliographical references and index.
ISBN 0-8061-3780-0 (alk. paper)
1. Lewis, Meriwether, 1774–1809—Death and burial. I. Holmberg, James J. (James John), 1958– II. Buckley, Jay H. III. Title.
F592.7.L42G85 2006
973.4′6092—dc22

2005055976

1 2 3 4 5 6 7 8 9 10

# Contents

# Illustrations

## Figures

## Map

# Foreword

## ELLIOTT WEST

In darker moments I sometimes wonder whether we require our most favored historical characters to die in particular ways. Abraham Lincoln, John Kennedy, Martin Luther King, even Elvis Presley: Their extraordinary accomplishments are not enough. We elevate their lives from merely remarkable to mythic only if those lives end with a poignant heroism or irony that makes the deaths somehow fitting, and even (as loathe as we might be to admit it) satisfying. We insist on a final sacrifice.

Meriwether Lewis is a lesser light than Lincoln or King (or that other Memphis fatality, *the* King), but it is still worth asking whether the story of his and William Clark's expedition would have had quite so powerful a grip on us if Lewis had died in bed at eighty or had fallen from the riverboat and drowned before starting on his journey up the Natchez Trace, the trip that ended with his death in the early morning of 11 October 1809. Certainly readers with a general interest in the expedition are much more likely to know something of Lewis's demise than of Clark's many later accomplishments and his peaceful death at sixty-eight, nearly three decades after Lewis's passing.

Lewis died violently and in the midst of controversy and emotional storm, which makes his sad, unsettling end line up with his troubled character and turbulent life. The place and time add a painful, delicious irony. He died along a well-traveled (if notorious) road just a few years after completing an epic journey on which he survived daredeath escapes from Indians and grizzlies.

And then there is the mystery. When the news of his death broke, everyone close to Lewis presumed he had taken his own life, but soon enough doubts were raised. Over the years the doubts have persisted, and during the past several years the question has found a new vigor: suicide or murder?

This book gives you an able introduction to the debate and presents arguments from both sides. It follows up with a judicious commentary on the ongoing spat, then lays out some of the basic documents so you can consider the evidence and judge for yourself.

Such a combination should appeal to three sorts of readers. First, those who have followed the question over the years will find here exceptionally fine summaries of both sides, as argued by John Guice and James Holmberg. Guice, a historian of the Old Southwest who is currently researching the story of the Natchez Trace, thoughtfully critiques the essential claims of those who say Lewis took his own life. He brings us up-to-date with key points raised on a recent well-received panel of the Southern Historical Association—the inspiration for putting this book together. Holmberg, editor of the letters from William Clark to his brother Jonathan, details the reasons why Clark, arguably the person who best knew Lewis's state of mind, was sure his friend died a suicide. Holmberg marshals as well the other sources that point toward that conclusion. In his commentary, Jay Buckley, author of an upcoming study of Clark's important work as Indian agent, stands between the two advocates, elaborates on what they say, and assesses each one's strengths and weaknesses. And finally, for any questions about how both sides are using the evidence, there are the documents to consult.

The most impassioned Lewis and Clark junkie will surely take away a better understanding of the incident and the issues—and will probably find some new insights as well. I certainly did. A good example is a point made by Clay Jenkinson in his introduction. Both a scholar of the Jefferson years and a historical reenactor of both Lewis and Jefferson, Jenkinson draws on his command of the documentary record. He points to a letter written by Lewis shortly before his death and in the wake of the scandal surrounding Aaron Burr's shenanigans on Lewis's political turf, the lower Mississippi valley. Lewis seems to allude to accusations of his involvement in treasonous conspiracies. This was an age when personal honor, to put it mildly, weighed more heavily in the scales of reputation than is the case with people in the public eye today, and the rumors seem to have stung Lewis painfully. How much, we can wonder, did they further upset his unstable personality?

It's an example of how another audience—general readers and students new to western and early American history—can enjoy and learn from this collection. The bloody events at Grinder's Stand and the facts of Lewis's situation, when we pick them apart, open wide a window onto the remarkable years when the republic was, paradoxically, both starting to come into focus and changing rapidly. The expedition itself, of course, was a revelation of Americans' expanding vision of themselves and of their first, tentative relations with the Far West and its peoples. Lewis's troubles are a case study in the era's cutthroat politics and the nature of political networking. Questions about John Pernier and James Neelly easily broaden into questions about the shadowy side of black-white relations in the South. Pernier, like York in his later years, was a freedman, a status with its own special vulnerabilities. How might he have seen his situation, square in the midst of a highly visible mess and dealing with a dodgy character like Neelly? The site of the tragedy, along the Natchez Trace, the bandit-ridden "Devil's Backbone," tempts us into another dark corner of Jeffersonian America—the violence that was chronic across the young nation and at its worst in the restless, loosely governed region where Lewis died.

Finally, and more broadly yet, this book might be a primer for anyone interested in how historians work. If nothing else, it makes one thing clear: We are an argumentative bunch. Nobody reading these pages could possibly think of history as a cut-and-dried record of the past, or of historians as people who simply write down what is obvious in the evidence. The record itself is slippery. A key document seeming to support the claims of suicide is Gilbert Russell's statement from 1811. But it seems to be in someone else's hand, so is it really Russell's or the work of someone trying to throw us off the trail? At certain points Mrs. Grinder's testimony has us furrowing our brows. Accounts of Lewis on the eve of his trip describe him as disturbed, even "deranged," but could they be describing the throes of malaria rather than a fatal mental unraveling? The possibilities of forgery and exaggeration lead to another set of questions, those of motive, that further muddy the evidence. Did Grinder and Neelly have something to hide? Did Russell and others have their own political reasons to put the whole business behind them as quickly as possible?

Just as pertinent, and more uncomfortable, are questions for ourselves. Is there something in *us* that resists believing that a man like Lewis could choose such a sordid end? Something that wants to turn a pathetic, lunatic moment into what is more dramatic and understandable—murder most foul? And ultimately, of course, questions of motive take us into the trickiest terrain of all, Lewis's own mind. Advocates of murder point out all the reasons Lewis had to live; advocates of suicide observe that someone who kills himself is not acting within reason. Guice quotes a California gunsmith's take on the fact that Lewis supposedly needed two shots to finish himself off. This fellow doubted the ability of anyone to shoot himself twice with this particular weapon, for according to him, "the learning curve . . . would be quite nearly vertical." It's a great line, but it begs the question. A learning curve applies to rational persons, not those intent on self-destruction.

The arguments and documents between these covers, then, let us see the business of history for what it is—part advocacy, part forensics, part psychology, a mix of reasoned analysis, intuition, and self-reflection. The lesson is all the more enjoyable because its occasion is such a great story. Let's face it: Whether Meriwether Lewis, our troubled hero, took his own life or fell at the hands of others, it is his violent death, as ambiguous and impenetrable as Lewis's own character, that keeps him alive in our collective memory.

# Preface

## JOHN D. W. GUICE

Late in the afternoon on 10 October 1809 one of the nation's great heroes reined his horse off the Natchez Trace to spend the night at Grinder's Stand. The rustic homestead consisted of two rough-hewn log cabins a few paces apart and a distant barn. It was a pleasant fall day some seventy miles southwest of Nashville, Tennessee. What occupied Meriwether Lewis's mind we will never know, but we do know that shortly after sunup the next morning he died there. Who held the weapon or weapons that fired the fatal shots during the night? Did Lewis take his own life or did an assassin? After nearly two centuries, this remains one of the most fascinating, puzzling, and enduring questions in all of American history.

Suicide or murder? What difference does it make? A lot of difference to historians concerned with the integrity of their profession, to Americans who expect accuracy in their nation's written history, and to members of the Lewis family who still refuse to accept the report of suicide. In addition, this question offers an intriguing study in historiography. Why do some highly respected historians adamantly insist that Lewis shot himself, yet others argue just as vehemently that someone murdered him?

In his introduction, Clay Jenkinson, in his inimitable style, explores the depth and breadth of this historiographical challenge. Then two of the following essays present opposing viewpoints based on the latest scholarship. A third and final essay offers a balanced and unbiased analysis of the strengths and weaknesses of the arguments presented for both suicide and murder. Barring the appearance of conclusive scientific evidence obtained through a forensic examination of Lewis's remains, the question of homicide or suicide will remain one of America's most perplexing mysteries. Meanwhile, this book allows readers to sit as a jury, so to speak, and to arrive at their own private verdicts after seeing both positions.

Such a comprehensive study of Lewis's death is long overdue, especially since the bicentennial of his demise is virtually upon us. Indeed, nearly two generations have passed since Vardis Fisher addressed this mystery in his 1962 book *Suicide or Murder?* and new evidence supporting both sides of the question has emerged. In addition, the debate intensified during the past decade as the Lewis family descendants futilely attempted, with forensic scientists representing them, to resolve the issue through an examination of his remains—a procedure that might determine whether his death was a homicide or a suicide. Hence the status of the debate over the manner of Lewis's death accents the timeliness of this anthology, which should serve as the authoritative treatment of the topic for the foreseeable future.

Despite the intensity of this debate and despite varying interpretations of the meaning of certain events, proponents of both views agree on certain basic facts relating to the life of Meriwether Lewis between the Lewis and Clark Expedition's return from the Pacific on 23 September 1806 and Lewis's arrival back in St. Louis as governor of Upper Louisiana Territory on 8 March 1808.[1] These facts include:

- An adoring public saluted and feted Lewis and his co-captain, William Clark, as they made their way from St. Louis to the Atlantic seaboard in a manner not seen since the inauguration of George Washington. But no one awaited their triumphant arrival with greater anticipation and excitement than President Thomas Jefferson. As a measure of his appreciation for their heroic accomplishments, Jefferson rewarded Lewis with the governorship of Upper Louisiana and appointed Clark brigadier general of the militia and principal Indian agent for the same territory. Simultaneously, the president named Frederick Bates as territorial secretary, a decision that soon brought Lewis immeasurable grief.

- Though Jefferson signed his gubernatorial commission on 3 March 1807, Governor Lewis did not arrive at his post until

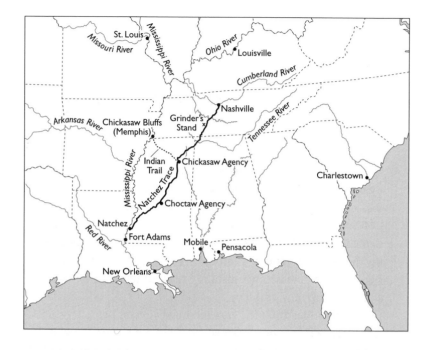

*The Fateful Route. On this map one can follow Meriwether Lewis's trip down the Mississippi River to Chickasaw Bluffs (Memphis), then down an Indian trail to the Natchez Trace, up the trace, and across the Tennessee River to Grinder's Stand. Based on a map by Mark Gunn, Meridian, Mississippi.*

8 March 1808—one year and five days later. Why the delay? As will be shown later, historians are not in accord as to the precise answer. Indeed, the explanations for his tardiness are subject to speculation.

• While interpretations of the effectiveness of Lewis's role as governor vary, there is general agreement on the sequence of events that brought him to Grinder's Stand. His problems related directly to the change in federal policies and personnel after James Madison replaced Thomas Jefferson in the White House. Governor Lewis was so preoccupied with the complexity of territorial affairs that evidently he gave little thought to these changes until the War Department refused to honor a five-hundred dollar expense related to the return of the Mandan chief Big White (Sheheke) and his family to their people up the Missouri River. Personally responsible for unauthorized expenditures, Lewis instantly realized that now he faced a serious cash flow problem.

• On 4 September 1809 the enraged Lewis, accompanied by his free black servant John Pernier, boarded a boat for New Orleans to begin a sea voyage to Washington to straighten out matters with the parsimonious War Department bureaucracy. At New Madrid, Lewis went ashore and wrote a will designating his mother as his sole beneficiary. By the time he reached Fort Pickering at Chickasaw Bluffs, the site of present-day Memphis, Lewis was too ill to proceed downstream. Captain Gilbert C. Russell, commander at the fort, placed Lewis under the care of his surgeon's mate, who prescribed abstention from whiskey but allowed consumption of wine.

• While resting at Fort Pickering, Lewis decided that it was too dangerous to attempt a sea voyage, because he could not risk the loss of the expedition journals that were among his baggage. Another visitor at the fort was James Neelly, a former militia major who was then Chickasaw Indian agent. Two weeks after his arrival at Fort Pickering, the governor and his servant Pernier, together with Neelly and his slave, headed south along an Indian trail toward the Chickasaw Agency on the Natchez Trace. Originally a series of interconnecting Indian trails, the Natchez Trace in 1809 was still an unimproved wilderness road that ran approximately 550 miles from Natchez on the Mis-

sissippi River northeastward through the Choctaw and Chickasaw Indian nations to Nashville on the Cumberland River.
From there other roads led to the Ohio Valley and the Atlantic
seaboard.

- Heavily armed, the governor carried a rifle, two pistols, a dirk,
  and a tomahawk. Strapped on a packhorse were two trunks
  and a portfolio containing the sixteen leather-bound journals.
  The party rested two days at the Chickasaw Agency before
  heading northeastward up the increasingly hilly Natchez Trace
  toward the Tennessee River. When they camped a day's ride
  beyond the river on 9 October, two horses disappeared during
  the night. Governor Lewis and the two servants continued up
  the trace while Major Neelly remained behind to search for the
  horses. Neelly, therefore, was absent when Lewis reined his
  horse off the trail to spend the night of 10 October at Grinder's
  Stand.[2]

## Notes

1. For a more detailed account of Lewis's activities between 1806 and his
arrival at Grinder's Stand on the Natchez Trace in 1809, see Guice, "Fatal
Rendezvous" (1998).

2. Descendants of the owner of this "stand," or inn, contend that Griner is
the proper spelling, though in many contemporary and historical accounts it is
spelled Grinder. Because most accounts use the place-name Grinder's Stand,
we do also.

# Acknowledgments

One of my favorite historians of the American West, Walter Prescott Webb, once wrote a rather humorous essay on the writing of prefaces. His pieces invariably were entertaining—even one about the Coca-Cola machine outside his office at the University of Texas. Unfortunately, Webb offered no advice regarding acknowledgments. I wish he had, for this is a serious matter, and we approach it with the knowledge that we will inevitably overlook someone deserving of recognition. Perhaps that is why many acknowledgments are brief and general. Even so, we must single out a few special people among the countless men and women who have assisted us. Jim Holmberg and Jay Buckley contribute their own expressions of gratitude after mine.

First I offer my blanket expression of thanks to the program committees of the Western History Association and the Southern Historical Association who, over the past decade, expressed their confidence in the value of sessions on the death of Meriwether Lewis, and to the numerous program chairs of regional societies who followed suit. And to those persons who chaired such sessions, even when they strongly disagreed with my point of view, I offer my sincere thanks.

I am compelled to mention just a few who encouraged my research and who helped make this book possible. I am deeply indebted to James E. Starrs, professor of law and professor of forensic sciences at George Washington University, for inviting me to testify at the 1996 coroner's inquest in Hohenwald, Tennessee, and for arranging my appearance at a 1997 meeting of the American Association of Forensic Sciences in New York City. It is important to mention that I began my work and publications on Lewis's death before I became aware of Professor Starrs' interest in the exhumation of Lewis's remains, and that I had concluded, before we personally met, that a forensic examination of those remains was essential for the integrity of American history.

Of course, there is no way to adequately express my appreciation to Elliott West and Clay Jenkinson for contributing the foreword and introduction, respectively. Both are graceful stylists and provocative, creative thinkers. To Jim Holmberg I owe a special thank you for his courtesies when I researched at the Filson Historical Society in Louisville, Kentucky, for his willingness to share the session entitled "The Mysterious

Death of Meriwether Lewis" at the Southern Historical Association meeting in Houston, Texas, in 2003, and for his excellent contribution to this book. My much younger colleague Jay Buckley was also kind enough to participate in the same session; to write his creative analysis of the two sides of this historiographical debate; and to compile and assemble all of the essays, the table, and the bibliography for this book.

Mark Gunn, one of my former graduate students who teaches at Meridian (Mississippi) Community College, helped me in a host of ways. Among other things, he traveled the Natchez Trace with me to photograph its many important sites, including the one at Grinder's Stand where the State of Tennessee erected the monument over Meriwether Lewis's grave nearly a century before construction of the Natchez Trace Parkway began. I join my co-authors in thanking J. Frederick Fausz for granting permission to revise and add information to his table that originally appeared in a 2003–2004 special issue of *Gateway Heritage: Quarterly Magazine of the Missouri Historical Society*; that table appears as an appendix to this book.

All three of us are particularly indebted to Charles Rankin, editor-in-chief of the University of Oklahoma Press, who had the vision to pursue and believe in the merits of this publication project after he chaired our SHA session. Simply put, without his active support, this anthology would not be in your hands. While we appreciate the entire Press staff, special recognition is due editorial assistant Bobbie Canfield, associate editor Steven Baker, and managing editor Alice Stanton. We also thank Ursula Smith, copyeditor, and Ernie Price of the National Park Service for their input and interest.

Finally, words cannot express appropriately my gratitude for the support and encouragement of my wife, Nancy, a talented artist and creative writer.

JDWG

I offer my thanks to some of the same people as do my colleagues John Guice and Jay Buckley. It was a pleasure to work on this project with John and Jay. I enjoyed delving deeper into an enduring historical mystery that has intrigued me for years. Our discussions of Meriwether Lewis's tragic death were both enjoyable and enlightening, and I hope that the reader will find our essays to be so as well. Chuck Rankin at the University of Oklahoma Press saw the potential for a book after moderating the SHA session and encouraged John, Jay, and me to expand our papers into a manuscript. John took on the job of shepherding us along, and Jay, with his much greater computer ability, merged our individual papers together into one cohesive work. The obvious team effort of this book extends to those who provided assistance in a variety of ways. Thank you to the Filson Historical Society for providing illustrations of letters and newspapers. My thanks to Tom Kanon of the Tennessee State Library and Archives, Anthony Tedeschi of Indiana University's Lilly Library, Dennis Northcott of the Missouri Historical Society, and David Mattern of the Papers of James Madison project at the University of Virginia for their archival assistance. And of course no thanks would be complete without acknowledging the continuing support of my wife, Ruthe, and children, Elise, Aaron, and Emily. They have grown quite accustomed to my absences in both mind and body as I go about my "Clarking," as it has become known. What I do wouldn't be possible without their support.

JJH

It is always nice to be able to get in the last word, especially when they are kind ones. I, too, have enjoyed working with John Guice, Jim Holmberg, Elliott West, and Clay Jenkinson on this book. Editor Charles Rankin and the staff at the University of Oklahoma Press have been helpful and professional. I express my gratitude to John Buckley, Josh Campbell, Julie Harris, Von Memory, Larry Morris, William Swagerty, and Elliott West for reading and commenting on versions of my chapter. I thank Jill Jackson, former curator of the William P. Sherman Library and Archives, and I am grateful for the generous assistance I received from the staffs at the Lewis and Clark Trail Heritage Foundation and the Lewis and Clark National Historic Trail Interpretive Center, all located in Great Falls, Montana. Thanks as well to James Starrs for making additional research items available to me. I am also grateful for the encouragement I have received from David Magleby, Neil York, and my colleagues at Brigham Young University. I appreciate the encouragement of my wife, Becky, and I thank my children, David, Mary, and Jared, for sharing their father with Lewis and Clark.

JHB

# By His Own Hand?

# Meriwether Lewis's Mysterious Death on the Natchez Trace

## CLAY JENKINSON

Nobody doubts that Meriwether Lewis, the governor of Upper Louisiana Territory, died of gunshot wounds in the early morning hours of 11 October 1809 at a rude inn on the Natchez Trace, approximately seventy miles from Nashville, Tennessee.

He was thirty-five years old and still, though diminished, an American hero.

There were no direct eyewitnesses. The three quasi-witnesses—Priscilla Grinder, the proprietor of the inn; James Neelly, an Indian agent to the Chickasaw nation; and Lewis's free black servant John Pernier—all reported that Lewis had shot himself once in the head and also in the abdomen. They were, as seems likely, either convinced that Lewis had indeed committed suicide, or they were engaged in a conspiracy to explain or cover up the murder of Governor Lewis. Most historians now support the view that Lewis committed suicide, but a determined minority find the suicide story implausible and insist that, in effect, the case needs to be reopened. The call for a renewed investigation is the business of this book.

*Meriwether Lewis by Charles Willson Peale, 1807. Courtesy Independence National Historical Park.*

At his untimely death, Lewis's life was in disarray. He was probably ill—of malaria and perhaps other maladies. His personal finances were a deteriorating mess. Three months prior, on 15 July 1809, he had been formally rebuked for unauthorized territorial expenditures by the secretary of war, William Eustis, who made sure that Lewis understood that "[the] President [James Madison] has been consulted and the observations herein contained have his approval." Lewis had made a number of enemies in St. Louis, the most outspoken of whom was his subordinate, the territorial secretary Frederick Bates. Lewis appears to have made no headway on his projected three-volume account of the Voyage of North Western Discovery, and he had failed to keep his patron, Thomas Jefferson, apprised of his lack of progress. Lewis's epistolary silence, some of it pertaining to pressing territorial business, was remarked by everyone, often in terms of great frustration. Unlike his "partner in discovery," William Clark, Lewis had been unable to find a wife. Nor had he found reentry into normal "civilized" life either smooth or satisfying. To make matters worse, Lewis seems also to have believed that he was in danger of being formally recalled by the U.S. government. The distinguished man who appeared at Grinder's Stand about sunset on 10 October 1809 was both mentally troubled and physically impaired.

We know that Meriwether Lewis was on his way east (probably to Albemarle County, Virginia, certainly to Washington, D.C.) to try to sort out his gubernatorial difficulties and to redeem his reputation and honor with the War Department and President Madison. It seems likely, too, that he intended to make a dramatic (albeit belated) attempt to see his travel journals through to press—or to find someone in Philadelphia who could help him achieve that goal.

The bulk of the available evidence seems to point overwhelmingly toward suicide. Lewis's two closest associates, his friend William Clark and his patron Thomas Jefferson, were shocked but not surprised to hear the news, and so far as we know neither one of them ever found reason to revise his initial understanding that the death of their mercurial friend had been at his own hands.

Clark's reaction was unambiguous. In a letter to his brother Jonathan, dated 28 October 1809, Clark wrote, "I fear this report has too much truth, tho' hope it may have no foundation. . . . I fear O! I fear the waight of his mind has over come him, what will be the Consequence?" (See Document 5 in Documents section for full text.) Clark, in short, understood that Lewis was a mentally troubled man and that in that state of mind he had taken his own life.

Four years later, on 18 August 1813, on what would have been Lewis's thirty-ninth birthday, Thomas Jefferson penned for publication a biographical sketch of his former secretary. He was emphatic that Lewis had committed suicide: "About 3. oclock in the night he did the

*William Clark by Charles Willson Peale, 1810. Courtesy Independence National Historical Park.*

deed which plunged his friends into affliction and deprived his country of one of her most valued citizens." Jefferson, who was a preternaturally cautious man, and highly protective of his protégés, did not, in the official publication of the expedition's journals, express the slightest doubt that Lewis had taken his own life.

*Thomas Jefferson by Charles Willson Peale, 1791–1792. Courtesy Independence National Historical Park.*

James Neelly, the most authoritative individual at the scene of the shooting, left no room for ambiguity in the 18 October 1809 letter he sent to Jefferson in which he reported the death of Governor Lewis. The letter opened, "It is with extreme pain that I have to inform you of the death of His Excellency, Meriwether Lewis, Governor of upper Louisiana who died on the morning of the 11th Instant and I am sorry to say by suicide." Later in the letter, Neely acknowledged that he was working from hearsay. "The woman [Priscilla Grinder] reports that about three o'clock she heard two pistols fire off in the Governors Room. the servants being awakined by her, came in but too late to save him. he had shot himself in the head with one pistol & a little below the Breast with the other." (See Document 4 for full text.)

In the second of two accounts he provided concerning the death of Lewis, Captain Gilbert Russell of Fort Pickering at today's Memphis, Tennessee, not only added his authority to the suicide account, but asserted that on Lewis's descent from St. Louis to Fort Pickering by boat on the Mississippi River, the governor had twice attempted suicide. On 26 November 1811 Russell wrote, "[T]he Commanding officer of the Fort [Pickering] on discovering his situation, and learning from the Crew that he had made two attempts to Kill himself, in one of which he had nearly succeeded, resolved at once to take possession of him and his papers, and detain them there untill he recovered, or some friend might arrive in whose hands he could depart in Safety." (See Document 9 for full text.) Every student of the Lewis and Clark Expedition wishes that Russell had provided more detail about these alleged suicide attempts, including an explanation of why they miscarried.

Eighteen months after the shooting, the ornithologist Alexander Wilson visited Grinder's Stand on a tour he was making through America to promote a multivolume publication project he was undertaking. Wilson appeared at Lewis's gravesite sometime in the first months of 1811. Lewis and Wilson had become friends in Philadelphia in 1807 during the period in which Lewis was actively involved in lining up illustrators, engravers, scientific analysts, and printers for his projected publication project. At that time, Lewis had commissioned Wilson to make "drawings of such of the feathered tribes as had been preserved and were new" from the expedition, including the western tanager, Clark's nutcracker, and Lewis's woodpecker.

After an emotionally draining interview with Priscilla Grinder, Wilson wrote, "I took down from Mrs. Grinder the particulars of that melancholy event, which affected me extremely." (See Document 8 for full text.) He visited the gravesite, gave innkeeper Robert Grinder funds to improve and maintain the grave, wept alone in the "gloomy and savage wilderness which I was just entering alone," and composed a rather fine elegy for his fallen friend.

That Meriwether Lewis's friend and advocate Alexander Wilson, a man of precision and scientific method, made the long journey to the gravesite to pay his last respects and to investigate the circumstances of Lewis's death, interviewed the principals, and came away convinced that Lewis had committed suicide would seem to be a nearly insurmountable problem for the murder theorists. Wilson would certainly have been alert to any prevarication or improbability, slyness or inconsistency in the testimony of Priscilla Grinder and other Natchez Trace provincials, and yet he came away convinced that Lewis had taken his own life. If any contemporary might be counted on to have cracked open the case, and announced the possibility that it was something more sinister than suicide, it would have been Wilson. (So far as we know, William Clark never visited the site.) And yet Alexander Wilson's visit to Grinder's Stand confirmed, rather than disturbed, the suicide account.

All of this contemporary testimony would seem to make the case for suicide conclusive, except for two extremely significant problems. (1) So far as we know, nobody actually witnessed the shootings that led to Lewis's death. (2) The suicide story depends heavily on the testimony of James Neelly, who is not necessarily a reliable reporter, in part because, according to his own account, he was not present at Grinder's Stand at the time of the shooting. Neelly had only recently (July 1809) been appointed a federal Indian agent to the Chickasaw nation. Contrary to some opinion, he was not a friend of Meriwether Lewis's. He was not altogether honorable in his handling of Lewis's personal property in the years following his death, and he was dismissed from his post in 1812. Lewis's friend Gilbert Russell, in his account of 26 November 1811, actually blamed Neelly for Lewis's demise, because he believed that Neelly had encouraged Lewis to drink at a time when his only hope was strict sobriety. Although none of these facts necessarily impeaches Neelly's testimony, his character is sufficiently problematic to open the door to alternative theories concerning the death of Governor Lewis.

For the record, I acknowledge that I believe that Meriwether Lewis committed suicide. But there are enough perplexities in the documentary record to invite doubt and to suggest that humility, rather than certainty, is the proper response to what remains one of the principal mysteries of the Lewis and Clark Expedition.

The fact that nobody has ever made a convincing case for murder does not rule out the possibility that it *was* murder. On the one hand, it seems to me that no responsible historian can dismiss the idea that

Meriwether Lewis committed suicide. The evidence, however imperfect, lines up, and what we know about the character of Meriwether Lewis, and what Jefferson and Clark knew about the character of Meriwether Lewis, does not make his suicide implausible, nor—judging from their testimony—even unlikely. At the same time it seems to me that no responsible historian can rule out the possibility (however slender) that Lewis was murdered. We simply don't know enough about Lewis's last days or the precise sequence of events that occurred at Grinder's Stand on 10–11 October 1809 to rule out the possibility that Lewis was murdered. Nobody, it seems to me, can deny that there is an atmosphere of mystery and miasma surrounding the last days and death of Lewis, and that we would need to know much more to be fully confident in settling the case.

The murder theorists rightly assert that none of the "witnesses" actually saw the shooting. Some have gone so far as to reconstruct lunar cycles to prove that Mrs. Grinder could not have witnessed much on the moonless night of 10–11 October 1809. Murder advocates point out inconsistencies in the three separate accounts provided over a thirty-year span by Priscilla Grinder. They point in particular to the strange third interview, given in 1839, in which Mrs. Grinder appears to provide new evidence that points toward the possibility of murder. The character and actions of James Neelly are routinely viewed with suspicion by the murder theorists, and Lewis's free black servant Pernier is often cast in a less-than-favorable light. Some have suggested that key documents may be forgeries—or at least unreliable, given the amount of time that elapsed between the events in question and their penning. Everyone emphasizes how much of the suicide story rests on the testimony of two persons, James Neelly and Priscilla Grinder. In other words, what might appear to be a proliferation of suicide documentation is in fact highly derivative, and the sources are not unimpeachable.

The murder theorists argue for one of two scenarios: Either Lewis was murdered more or less randomly, as a clearly distinguished traveler, a man of means, stopping for the night at a crude inn on a trail that was not yet free of banditry; or some combination of Pernier, Neelly, and unnamed others killed Lewis for reasons that are not altogether clear but may have something to do with political conspiracy. That there is no significant fund of evidence to support either of these scenarios has not inhibited their advocates. Conspirators in a murder plot, so the argument goes, are not prone to leave incriminating documents. And of course it is possible that further investigation will unearth new documents of significance in the case. One of the weaknesses of the murder theory is that its advocates are willing to drop down to the random-murder scenario when the argument for conspiracy breaks down in academic or public debate.

A few have even gone so far as to suggest that Jefferson declared that Lewis committed suicide in his 1813 biographical statement, not because he was really convinced that it was true but because he had something to hide. Perhaps he feared that a thorough investigation might recall Aaron Burr's machinations to the detriment of the former president's reputation. This is roughly equivalent to suggesting that Lyndon Johnson might have had something to do with the assassination of President Kennedy in 1963. Just because the theory is preposterous does not rule out the remote possibility that it could be true.

Murder theorists focus intense suspicion on Mrs. Grinder—and the intriguing fact that Robert Grinder was absent when Governor Lewis arrived at the inn—and on James Neelly, who (as events later proved) was not a man of sterling integrity and who stole (or did not promptly return) a number of personal effects in Lewis's possession at the time of his death.

Doubts surrounding the suicide theory rest largely on two issues—one practical and one imponderable:

1. How is it that an expert gunman like Meriwether Lewis puts a pistol to his head, fires it, but fails to kill himself? Even if, as the suicide advocates argue, the first ball only grazed his skull, or penetrated it without doing terminal damage to his brain, would Lewis have had the presence of mind to fire a second (ultimately lethal) ball from a second pistol into his abdominal cavity? In other words, assuming that Lewis intended to kill himself, one would expect him to have been able to do so with a sureness and dispatch that are missing in the accounts we possess. It is not impossible to conceive that Lewis could put a gun to his head and fail to succeed, given the length of the pistols and the awkwardness of shooting toward himself rather than toward a creature before him. (It is the same difficulty one faces in trying to take a photograph of oneself at arm's length.) We can even assume that he was ill, deranged, intoxicated, or at least nervous. But still there is a sort of

bungling quality to the accounts we have of the suicide that seems out of character.

2. On a more philosophical and psychological plane, why would the man who discovered the Great Falls of the Missouri, who drank from the source of the "mighty and heretofore deemed endless Missouri River," the American Columbus, our own Captain Cook, now the young and promising governor of a western territory he helped to explore—what reason would such a man have to take his own life? Lewis's problems, though considerable, were by no means unique. The vouchers of other territorial officials (including William Clark, Gilbert Russell, and James Neelly, among others) were routinely challenged by penny-pinching and faraway Washington bureaucrats. Other explorers, including James Cook, a man much admired by Lewis, routinely employed men of letters to assist them in their publication projects. Jefferson himself was one of America's premier men of letters, with a network of friends in Philadelphia who could surely have helped Lewis complete his book. Indeed, Jefferson, Lewis's mentor and friend, had spent his whole life addressing seemingly impossible problems. If anyone could solve Lewis's problems, that person was the Sage of Monticello.

There have been calls by a number of individuals and groups to exhume Lewis's body in order to conduct forensic tests on the remains. The National Park Service, which administers the gravesite, has declined to permit the exhumation, and there is no likelihood that such permission will be granted in the future. Like it or not, historians, buffs, and conspiracy theorists are stuck with the slender and puzzling documentary evidence and the cautious speculative tools of the humanities. From this base alone, they must solve this mystery—assuming that it can ever be solved. But analysis is as good a historical tool as the shovel.

This much is certain. The idea that Meriwether Lewis was murdered on 11 October 1809 cannot be altogether ruled out.

Suicide advocates would prefer that Mrs. Grinder's story were more consistent over time; that James Neelly were a more admirable individual and had provided a more precise and thorough report about a man and matter of such importance; and that there had been an actual eyewitness to the shooting.

Murder advocates have a much greater burden. They must begin by discounting the testimony of James Neelly, John Pernier, Priscilla Grinder, and Gilbert Russell, among others. And then they must craft an alternative narrative for a story that is quite plausible in the form in which it has in fact come down to us. In other words, murder theorists must not only discredit the testimony of those closest to the actual events and provide motive for the conspiracy those individuals cobbled together in the hours after Lewis's death, but they must also account for the secondary reports and corroborations of men like Gilbert Russell and explain the ease with which Lewis's friends Thomas Jefferson and William Clark accepted the suicide story.

It is not quite clear what drives some people to prefer murder to suicide. Part of it, surely, is psychohistorical revulsion to the idea that Meriwether Lewis took his own life as a young and extremely promising man—and with his great task unfinished. There is no question that Lewis's apparent suicide casts an ominous shadow on what is, after all, one of the greatest and most successful stories in American history. The suicide shadow serves in an indefinable manner to deconstruct the larger Lewis and Clark story, to weaken its mythological scaffolding in a way that can be felt more easily than articulated. It both deepens and troubles the master narrative. It provides a potential subtext to a number of scenes from the journals, and it vaguely but certainly destabilizes the geopolitical project of the American republic in the first years of the nineteenth century. It even touches Jefferson somehow in our historic imagination. Lewis's suicide makes us all uneasy. The alternative notion that he was murdered by some frontier ruffian or some real or perceived enemy "explains" the events with fewer ramifications and less damage to Lewis's character, less erosion to America's continental project.

It is undeniable that much of the appeal of the murder theory has to do with the oddities, inconsistencies, logical problems, and unresolved issues of the suicide story as we possess it. For many who have puzzled over the documents and traced Lewis's last journey on maps or in the field, the account as we have it just doesn't ring true somehow. Unfortunately, the sense of misgiving is that vague.

The literature on the subject up till now has been unsatisfying. The arguments in standard biographies and standard treatments of the expedition are based on faith and hunches rather than on a careful sorting of the available evidence. Recently, most historians have adopted an aggressive commitment to the suicide scenario, with the implication that all serious discourse on this subject has thankfully come to an end. This would seem to me to be premature and somewhat irresponsible. Two books have been devoted specifically to the murder-suicide problem, and both are profoundly unsatisfactory. Vardis Fisher's *Suicide or Murder?* is essentially an advocate's brief (for murder) rather than a serious sifting of the evidence. David Chandler's *The Jefferson Conspiracies* is riddled with demonstrable historical errors, and, as in all conspiracy books, conjecture is piled on wild speculation on top of improbability to create a story that appears much more solid than in fact it is. Neither book does service to the murder-suicide debate, except to bring together some of the documents and all of the arguments, rational and insane.

What we need now are carefully researched articles and books that investigate the last days of Meriwether Lewis in the minutest detail: his itinerary, his associations, the people he encountered, the documents he produced, the items in his traveling kit, especially the medicines. Efforts must continue to be made to find the letter Lewis wrote to Clark sometime in September 1809, which Clark believed gave credence to the suicide report. "My reasons for thinking it possible," he wrote to Jonathan Clark on 28 October 1809, "is founded on the letter which I recved from him at your house."

A great deal more work needs to be done on the scope and the ramifications of the Aaron Burr conspiracy. In particular, we need to investigate the ways in which the activities of General James Wilkinson destabilized the already turbulent Missouri frontier in the years and months before Lewis's death. Whether Lewis was involved in actions that somehow (deliberately or inadvertently) touched the morass of Wilkinson-Burr machinations and maneuverings is unclear, but it cannot be ruled out, and it is certain that Lewis, like others, was caught up in the paranoia that swept through the western frontier during this volatile period.

The Burr conspiracy remains a mystery after two hundred years of intense scrutiny. Much of the mystery has to do with the indeterminacy of the political and economic dynamics of the deep interior of the continent in the years that surrounded the arrival of the nineteenth century. We see the trans-Appalachian region of this era through a glass darkly. It was in many respects a region beyond the matrix of law and due process. (That was part of the problem Lewis faced as a territorial governor.) It was a region characterized by intrigue, multiple and mixed motives, divided loyalties, overlapping and rival sovereignties, and unsettled and contested boundaries. A number of what we might call in the twenty-first century "economic development softwares" were running simultaneously when Lewis arrived in St. Louis in the spring of 1808, and it was by no means clear that he could successfully impose a Jeffersonian development plan on so remote and strong-willed a region. If Lewis had died violently in Philadelphia or Richmond, or for that matter within sight of Monticello, we would probably know much more about the circumstances of his death.

The key sentence in Lewis's outraged 18 August 1809 letter to Secretary of War William Eustis follows his denial that the expedition returning the Mandan leader Sheheke (Big White) to the Knife River villages in today's North Dakota intended to proceed on into the contested territory beyond the Rocky Mountains for unspecified purposes. "Be assured Sir, that my Country can never make 'A Burr' of me—She may reduce me to Poverty; but she can never sever my Attachment from her." This sentence raises two issues: First, it is not clear just what Lewis meant to imply here. Second, and more important, there is a world of signification behind this sentence that historians must investigate with great thoroughness if we wish to get to the heart of the mystery of Meriwether Lewis's last days.

There is mystery either way. If Lewis was murdered, the challenge now is to discover, if possible, who wanted him dead, and for what reason, and why virtually everyone close to the shooting chose to form a conspiracy to promote the suicide story. If, as seems more probable, Lewis took his own life at Grinder's Stand, the challenge is to determine why a man Thomas Jefferson would later declare possessed a panoply of "qualifications as if selected and implanted by nature in one body, for this express purpose"—why would such a man take his own life just three years after a triumphant journey into the heart of the North American continent?

The enduring attraction of the Lewis and Clark story lies precisely in the fact that it is not pat, that some key elements of the experience are unresolved. Though most people don't like to admit it, the fact that the leader of the nation's greatest journey of exploration was a strange man who continues to elude easy analysis and who died just three years after his triumphal return, under circumstances that continue to compel and perplex, is one source of the magic of the Lewis and Clark Expedition. Had Lewis lived on, like his more stable friend William Clark, and died quietly in his sleep sometime in the middle of the nineteenth century, one great source of the fascination of the Lewis and Clark Expedition would evaporate.

We are fortunate that one of America's greatest stories has fundamental mysteries at its core. Our duty as scholar-historians is to find, sort, and analyze all available evidence, but the glory of the humanities is that no matter what we turn (or dig) up, we can never pluck out the heart of the mystery of Meriwether Lewis.

# "I Fear the Waight of His Mind Has Over Come Him"

*The Case for Suicide*

## JAMES J. HOLMBERG

At a lonely Tennessee inn along the Natchez Trace on 11 October 1809, one of the greatest explorers in American history died. Meriwether Lewis, governor of Upper Louisiana Territory and co-leader of the famous 1803–1806 Lewis and Clark Expedition, died at Grinder's Stand some seventy miles southwest of Nashville. It was a violent death—a gunshot wound to the head and another to the body, with reported razor cuts to the arms, legs, and neck. Did this famous explorer die by his own hand? Or was he murdered? At the time of his death, the verdict was suicide. All recorded accounts pronounced it suicide, and no one disputed it.

There the matter lay for almost forty years. By the late 1840s a published report appeared stating that foul play had been involved in the governor's death. The report of the Lewis Monument Committee stated that "the impression has long prevailed that under the influence of disease of body and mind . . . Governor Lewis perished by his own hands. It seems more probable that he died by the hands of an assassin."[1] No evidence was cited, only the more likely possibility that it was murder.

What was it? Suicide or murder? Arguments for each have been presented for more than a century, facts and rumors gathered, evidence weighed, and conclusions espoused. Intelligent, thoughtful, and respected individuals have concluded for both suicide and murder. Arguments can be well researched, reasoned, and emotional. The nature of some murder theories is such that articles arguing for suicide are sometimes written simply to preserve the integrity and accuracy of the documents and of the facts of the case. Will we ever know what actually happened on that October night in Tennessee? Probably not, but we can use the sources available to us to theorize and reach reasoned and plausible conclusions. I believe that in the depths of depression and terrible emotional anguish Meriwether Lewis lost to an enemy that has defeated countless others—mental illness. That "dark despair"[2] overwhelmed him and seeing no way out, and perhaps wanting in some way to hurt the people who were hurting him, Lewis used a brace of pistols to end his life.

Will the murder-versus-suicide debate regarding Lewis's fate ever end? Probably not. Do those who believe Lewis committed suicide *want* to believe that? Of course not. Lewis is an American hero. Everyone would like to believe that this brave man, once capable of facing hostile Indians, grizzly bears, and the hardships and dangers of an epic journey, did not take his own life. But the sad truth is that he most likely did. Given certain conditions, anyone is capable of suicide. And at that time, and at that place, those conditions existed for Meriwether Lewis.

In the end, Lewis's inability to write the expedition's history extended to his inability to even leave a suicide note. Did he act rashly? On impulse? Or had he planned it out? After failing in earlier attempts at suicide on the boat, and later being put first under the crew's, then Russell's, and then Neelly's supervision—with Pernier a constant presence—was he determined to make another attempt on his life? Was telling Neelly to stay behind to look for the horses and then outpacing the servants an attempt to find solitude, or was it part of a plan based upon suicidal impulses? Was his letter of September 1809 to William Clark as close as he came to a declaration of his desire to leave this world?

We probably will never know the answers to these questions, but the best evidence is found in the contemporary reports concerning Lewis's postexpedition life and death. What do they reveal about Lewis and how convincing are they that Lewis took his own life? Those with Lewis in his last days as well as those who knew him best commented on the tragedy. Some of their views provide the sad details of the great explorer's downward spiral. From the accounts of Priscilla Grinder, James Neelly, John Pernier, and Gilbert Russell—all of whom were with Lewis in his last tortured weeks—to those of Thomas Jefferson, William Clark, and others who met the news of his suicide with sad acceptance, the contemporary sources tell a compelling and convincing story of a man who lost the battle with his inner demons and took his own life. An examination of this contemporary evidence results for most researchers in a conclusion of suicide. Documenting his difficult postexpedition life and spiral downward, ending in that isolated inn, is not pleasant, but it is where the evidence leads us.

When Captain Meriwether Lewis returned from the Pacific Ocean, he was one of the greatest heroes in the young nation's history. He was the subject of admiration and flattery. He even had a poem written about his exploits and fame. As Clay Jenkinson has so cogently written, Lewis was the unchallenged commander of a military unit for almost four years. His word was law. He perceived himself as the most important and interesting man in his world. In short, he had been a complete sovereign where no man—including William Clark—was perceived as his equal. But then came reentry into American society and politics. It was an adjustment Lewis couldn't make. Jenkinson and others have made the analogy of astronauts readjusting to the frustrations, tedium, and normalcy of life after having been to the moon—the "Buzz Aldrin syndrome." After all, when you've been to the moon, what's left? For Lewis it was much the same. After he and the Corps of Discovery had accomplished their mission, after what they had seen and experienced in the American West—its people, dangers, and wonders—what was left? For some there was plenty. For others, like Lewis, there was not.[3]

Lewis's failure to adjust and his tragic death can be traced to his procrastination in the East after having been appointed the governor of Upper Louisiana Territory, to his failure to form a serious romantic relationship, and to his failure to write the expedition history. To these can be added his political and financial setbacks, which served as the catalysts for a mental collapse. The arguments used by historians and medical professionals to explain what went wrong with Lewis after his return from the West include aspects of his personality and his mental profile. This information is crucial, for his perception of and reaction to events and people around him became the factors that pushed him to suicide. While we must be careful in assigning modern diagnoses to Lewis's documented symptoms, it is also appropriate that we do so. Theorizing that Lewis's hypochondria and melancholia would be diagnosed today as manic-depressive disorder helps explain why he turned a brace of pistols and a razor on himself.

The Corps of Discovery arrived in St. Louis on 23 September 1806. After discharging the men and wrapping up other duties, Lewis, Clark, York, and other corps members reached Louisville on 5 November. Lewis continued on without Clark from Louisville, spending Christmas with his family in Charlottesville and then reaching Washington by late December. He received a hero's welcome along his route. Washington society and the government lauded him and his accomplishments. He was honored with dinners and toasts. In early March 1807 he was appointed territorial governor of Upper Louisiana. Jefferson personally anointed him the person to write the expedition history, a work that in its concept would be one of the great contributions to science and travel literature. Consequently, Lewis arrived in Philadelphia in early April to arrange for work on the scientific findings and illustrations and to hire a publisher. Though he made a good start on the project, he stayed in Philadelphia longer than necessary. He knew he needed to return to Washington and then take up his new post in St. Louis. So why did he delay? Was he taking a holiday? Was he courting a prospective wife? Was he simply trying to recuperate—physically and mentally—from the rigors of the past four years? Lewis definitely enjoyed a busy social life. He attended three meetings of the American Philosophical Society and spent many an evening on the town. Both his accounts and the diary of his friend Mahlon Dickerson document drinking and social activity. The ladies also were an object of Lewis's attention, but nothing came of these dalliances. Jefferson expected Lewis to return to Washington by 4 July. Instead, it was late July before he left Philadelphia.[4] His tendency to procrastinate had been apparent from time to time on the expedition, when unexplained delays occurred. Was he again procrastinating? Was he trying to get the journals and notes in order so that he could begin writing the expedition narrative? Did he suffer from writer's block and put off the work? From the time he returned from the expedition until days before his death, Lewis talked of writing the book. But as far as is known, he never wrote one page of the manuscript. Why?

The publication of the expedition account and scientific discoveries would have assured Lewis's place in history and been lucrative financially. But others were beating him to it. Robert Frazer and Patrick Gass both advertised their forthcoming accounts of the expedition. Lewis had given Frazer permission to publish his journal but then reacted defensively and with hostility when Frazer actually moved ahead with plans for publication. (No publication ultimately appeared.) Gass's journal was published in 1807 and became an international best-seller. Apocryphal accounts also appeared using Lewis's and Clark's published reports and letters as well as excerpts from other travel accounts (not necessarily from the American West). Did the explorer believe that these works diminished the public's interest in his account? Did he believe the chance for even greater fame and rewards had been denied him? Was his sense of urgency to produce the history gone?

To this must be added the pressure of being Thomas Jefferson's handpicked author of the account. Its success lay in Lewis's hands. The president had definite ideas about how such a publication should be accomplished. He undoubtedly transmitted these opinions to Lewis. Jefferson was one of the most learned and accomplished men of his time. Did Lewis fear he would disappoint his mentor? It would certainly be intimidating to have someone of Jefferson's stature and ability critiquing your work. The president wrote to his scientist friends touting the importance and value of the work. He clearly was eager for its publication. But he was also the chief executive and had many other duties to occupy him. And he could be something of a dilettante. Did Jefferson lose some of his interest in the West after his curiosity had been satisfied and the Northwest Passage disproved? There was so much to be learned that Jefferson could have kept busy for years, but the initial energy had certainly waned. Did Lewis somehow perceive this and take it as a personal affront or rejection by his mentor?

The loss of expedition artifacts might have impeded progress on the book, causing Lewis more psychic damage than suspected. While Lewis was in Philadelphia, he received a letter from Jefferson, dated 4 June 1807, advising him that a shipment of expedition artifacts he was having transported from Washington to Richmond (and then on to Monticello) had been sunk and "every thing lost which water could injure." One can imagine Lewis's reaction to the news. His response to the president was moderate, but the sense of loss was palpable. "I sincerely regret the loss you sustained in the articles you shiped for Richmond," he wrote Jefferson on 27 June. "[I]t seems peculiarly unfortunate that those at least, which had passed the continent of America and after their exposure to so many casualties and wrisks should have met such destiny in their passage through a small portion only of the Chesapeak."[5]

The loss of these materials aside, Lewis's best course would have been to engage the services of an editor to assist him in writing the narrative. Not only would it have assured a style suitable for reading by the general public but doing so would have taken an immense burden off of him and gotten that fundamental part of the work started. Instead, he apparently always intended to write the account himself, something he obviously found impossible to do. Did he believe that he was the only one capable of writing the expedition history? Did he find it impossible to let an editor have the journals? Did he begin despairing by this time that he could actually write what Jefferson, his fellow members of the American Philosophical Society, and the public were clamoring for? He and Clark were bearing the financial burden of producing the book. Did the monetary demands with their consequent worries affect Lewis? Would things have turned out differently if Lewis had remained in the East until the book was done? Would he have produced a manuscript if he had been able to remain focused on the history's publication instead of taking up the responsibilities of territorial governor? Perhaps, but Jefferson needed someone he could trust in St. Louis, and Lewis was due a reward for his expedition success. In the end, that reward proved to be an important factor in the man's undoing.

Still needing to write the history, Lewis headed west in the winter of 1807–1808 to take up his duties in Upper Louisiana. In March 1808, when he arrived in St. Louis, all the work on the expedition history was apparently being done back in Philadelphia. That summer Lewis talked of returning east to finish writing the book. And for the next twelve months, he kept talking. Instead of working with the journals he had with him there in St. Louis, he continued to procrastinate. Even William Clark, who saw their financial opportunity fading, was unaware of Lewis's lack of progress. Queries from Jefferson about the progress of the book apparently served only to further immobilize him. There are many possibilities as to why Lewis failed to produce the expedition history but no definite answer.

Another factor cited in Lewis's postexpedition decline was his inability to find a wife. This failure seems puzzling. He should have had no shortage of marital prospects. Instead, women seemed to run from him. One woman actually left town to avoid him. Was he too intense in his attentions? Were his expectations too high? Did prospective mates dread life on the frontier? Lewis mentioned several women in regard to his determination to get a wife. Were any of these relationships truly serious? Some have theorized that he compared all women to his mother and found them lacking in some respect. Or that he talked about finding a wife but deep in his heart he did not want one and always found a reason to reject any possible mate.[6] This might or might not be true. It seems that a loving and supportive mate would have been important in helping to ground Lewis. He should have been able to find someone. But in the end he found no one.

Lewis's need to spend some time in the East before taking up his duties in St. Louis is understandable. But spending more than a year defies reason. Granted, there was much to be done before again turning westward. Debriefing Jefferson and other government officials, preparing the expedition history, and attempting to find a wife are all cited. Still, Lewis didn't reach St. Louis until March 1808. By contrast, William Clark, after he was appointed brigadier general of the Louisiana territorial militia and chief Indian agent of the territory in March 1807, was in St. Louis the following month. He had begun courting his future wife by January 1807 and was officially engaged by March. Clark would have long absences from St. Louis during his career, but he wasted no time in getting back to the West to plunge into his duties. It would seem that Lewis should also have been in a hurry to take up his duties. The territory was riven by factions competing for power, land, and riches. There was increasing unrest among the Natives as more traders and settlers ventured into Indian country. Lewis's territorial secretary, Frederick Bates, had acted as governor since his arrival in April 1807 and had built his political base. Lewis obviously had many reasons to be in St. Louis as quickly as possible. Instead he tarried in the East. For stretches of that time it is not known what he was doing. After his initial burst of activity regarding the book, he apparently did little, if anything. His letters to friends and associates were much fewer than would be expected. He reported bouts of illness, and it is known he was drinking. Was he slipping into that "habit" of alcoholism that Jefferson later lamented? In August 1807 he attended Aaron Burr's trial for treason in Richmond. He started west in November, passing through Fincastle, Virginia, where he visited Clark's fiancée, Julia Hancock, and her family and made one more failed attempt at courtship. He didn't arrive in Kentucky until January and spent at least a month there. It is almost as if

Lewis was avoiding his new life in St. Louis. Did he sense that this chapter in his life would be his last? Were his mental problems increasingly affecting his ability to function? Did he need more time to rest and recover from his journey? Was he overwhelmed by all that lay before him? There seems to be no single answer.

In March 1808 when Lewis finally did arrive in St. Louis, he was greeted with political feuds and alliances he was ill prepared to face. He and Bates were soon at odds and barely on speaking terms. Bates must be considered a biased source and his letters read with a degree of skepticism, but they are an important source in understanding Lewis's decline. On 15 April 1809, a year after Lewis's arrival in St. Louis, Bates offered his assessment of Lewis and his situation: "I lament the unpopularity of the Governor; but he has brought it on himself by harsh and mistaken measures. He is inflexible in error, and the irresistable Fiat of the People, has, I am fearful, already sealed his condemnation."[7]

In the months that followed, Lewis was a recurring subject in Bates's letters, and the increasingly distrustful and hostile nature of their relationship is obvious. Bates's 14 July 1809 letter to his brother Richard provides a view of this acrimonious relationship and Lewis's growing problems:

> Gov. Lewis leaves this [place] in a few days for Phila. Washingn. & c. He has fallen from the Public esteem & almost into the public contempt. He is well aware of my increasing popularity . . . and has for some time feared that I was at the head of a Party whose object it would be to denounce him to the President and procure his dismission. The Gov. is greatly mistaken in these suspicions; and I have accordingly employed every frank and open explanation which might have a tendency to remove that veil with which a few worthless fellows have endeavoured to exclude from him the sunshine.[8]

Bates also offered this assessment: "How unfortunate for this man that he resigned his commission in the army: His habits are altogether military & he never can I think succeed in any other profession."[9]

Lewis's situation continued to worsen that summer of 1809. His procrastination in going east was noted by both Bates and Clark. On 25 July Bates reported that "Gov. Lewis, with the best intentions in the world, is, I am fearful, losing ground. His late preparations for the Indian War have not been popular." He later wrote that he believed Lewis

*Frederick Bates. Engraving from John Thomas Scharf,* History of St. Louis City and County *(1883). Courtesy Missouri Historical Society.*

would not be nominated for a second term as governor and that he suffered from an "unhappy situation" and "mortifications."[10]

How Bates reacted to Lewis's death is chronicled in his 9 November letter to his brother. It also provides additional information and insight concerning Lewis. "I had no personal regard for him and a great deal of political contempt," Bates confessed. "Yet I cannot but lament, that after all his toils and dangers he should die in <u>such a manner</u>." He then reviewed his relationship with Lewis and the opinion he had formed of the governor. "He had been . . . over whelmed by so many flattering caresses of the <u>high & mighty</u>, that, like an overgrown baby, he began to think that everybody about the House must regulate their conduct to his caprices." By Bates's own assessment, Lewis disliked and distrusted him because he stood so tall in the public's estimation. This made cooperation and even civility between the two difficult, despite Bates's best efforts—according to Bates himself—and led to at least one public display of temper by Lewis at a ball. Bates recounted how he defended himself against claims that he had caused Lewis to become deranged, noted his own high public approval, and professed to have no design on replacing Lewis.[11]

In mid-August 1809 Lewis received a letter from Secretary of War William Eustis informing him that some of his invoices had been rejected. Not only did this precipitate the collapse of Lewis's personal finances, but he took the rejection as a denunciation by the Madison administration. With that letter from Eustis, his fragile mental state broke. In a maelstrom of fury and hurt, he wrote an emotional letter dated 18 August defending his actions as governor. He confessed that Eustis's letter caused feelings that were "truly painful" and hoped that his explanation would receive a "full and fair Investigation." The government's rejection of his vouchers had plunged him into a financial crisis but his faith in that government was unshaken: , "Be assured Sir," he wrote Eustis, "that my Country can never make 'A Burr' of me—She may reduce me to Poverty; but she can never sever my Attachment from her." He was coming to Washington in person to prove his integrity, leadership, and ability to continue as governor of Louisiana. The matter was too involved and the charges too serious to try to resolve by letter. Therefore, he told Eustis, he would set out for Washington on 24 August.[12]

If Lewis suffered from manic-depressive disorder, as seems likely, this last setback sent him into a mental tailspin from which he would not recover. As he noted in his letter to Eustis, and as Clark and others commented, Lewis was trying to stave off financial collapse. Clark wasn't sure he could. And the eventual settlement of his estate would record the level of his debt.[13]

Lewis's whole world seemed to be crumbling. Politically, financially,

*William Eustis by Gilbert Stuart, c. 1806. Bequest of Eustis Langdon Hopkins, 1945. Courtesy Metropolitan Museum of Art.*

romantically, professionally, personally. Time seemed to be of the essence. He talked of going east immediately, and even Clark thought he had left on 25 August. But he apparently delayed until 4 September. Even on the brink of ruin, Lewis was a victim of the tendency to procrastinate that had periodically plagued him in the past.

So it was that with all these troubles burdening him, Lewis set out for

Washington, perhaps with some sense that he would never reach it. What happened in that first week on the Mississippi to spur him to write a will? It was reported in the St. Louis paper he was ill when the boat put in at New Madrid. And it was there, on 11 September, that he wrote his will. He also wrote William Clark. Was that letter akin to a suicide note? Clark later told his brother that Lewis's letter was one of the reasons he immediately accepted the report of his friend's death as a suicide. In any event, when Lewis reached Fort Pickering at the Chickasaw Bluffs on 15 September, he was under close watch by the boat's crew. It was reported that he had tried to kill himself twice and had nearly succeeded once. At the fort, the post commander, Gilbert Russell, took charge of him while he recovered from his "derangement." Lewis wrote another will while at Pickering. He also wrote to President Madison and to his army friend Amos Stoddard. His letter to Madison was written on 16 September, the day after he reached the Bluffs. That letter shows clear evidence of confused thought, with numerous strikeouts and insertions. Someone in his right senses would not have sent such a messy letter to the president. His letter of 22 September to Stoddard was more carefully written, reflecting an improved mental condition. But it also confesses his failure to answer several letters from Stoddard since Lewis's return from the expedition. Stoddard, like several others, including Jefferson, had been mystified and irritated by Lewis's silence.[14] (See Documents 2 and 3 in the Documents section.)

Those letters, the will, and a promissory note to Russell were apparently the last things that Lewis wrote. We must depend on the reports of others to learn his fate, and these reports tell us of his relapse after leaving Chickasaw Bluffs; of his wild imaginings that Clark was coming to his rescue and would make everything right; of his drinking and perhaps his abuse of medicines; and of James Neely's, John Pernier's, and Priscilla Grinder's alarm at his behavior. This all seems to be preamble to Meriwether Lewis's final decision that things were not going to get better and that death was the answer. It clearly was not a rational decision by a rational man. Lewis still had much to live for. It was possible that he would have been able to settle his difficulties with officials in Washington and continue as governor of Louisiana. It was possible that he could have gone to Philadelphia and made progress on writing the expedition history. He might even have found a wife, a helpmate who would have seen him through his times of despair.

But maybe Meriwether Lewis had stood as much as he could. After

*James Madison by Catherine A. Drinker, after Gilbert Stuart, 1875. Courtesy Independence National Historical Park.*

years of keeping his mental demons at bay, they had finally managed to breach his defenses. His episodes of derangement were becoming more frequent and more severe. It was harder and harder to climb out of that black pit of depression. He simply couldn't go on. Death would be a release. He would finally find peace while at the same time punishing those who had hurt and defamed him.

There are ten contemporary sources for the verdict that Meriwether Lewis killed himself. They can be separated into two groups: those who were with Lewis in the days before his death and those who knew Lewis and believed he was capable of suicide. In the first group are Gilbert Russell, Priscilla Grinder, James Neelly, and John Pernier. In the second are Captain John Brahan, William Clark, Thomas Jefferson, Alexander Wilson, an anonymous friend who wrote Lewis's obituary, and a whole cluster of people—from St. Louis to Washington and Philadelphia—who knew Lewis and overwhelmingly accepted the fact of suicide. Their concurrence appeared in various letters and newspaper reports in the weeks and months following Lewis's death. Nothing at the time, including statements by the Lewis and Meriwether families and reports coming out of Tennessee, contradicted the news that Lewis had taken his own life.

Lewis left no final words explaining why he killed himself. There is no voice from beyond the grave to guide us. In the absence of a declarative statement—a suicide note—and incontrovertible eyewitness proof, we must depend on the explorer's actions and statements and the statements and opinions of his contemporaries to guide us in examining the circumstances of his death.

In September 1809 Captain Gilbert Christian Russell was the commander of Fort Pickering. Russell came from the same social and patriotic Virginia background as Lewis and Clark. He joined the army in 1803, resigned in 1807, and rejoined in 1808 as a captain. He was honorably discharged in 1815 with the rank of colonel.[15] Russell was not the disreputable and shady character that some murder theorists claim when they include him as a suspect in Lewis's death.

On 15 September 1809 Russell received an unexpected guest in the person of Governor Meriwether Lewis. Traveling down the Mississippi to New Orleans, Lewis's boat put in at the Bluffs. Bound by the bonds of military brotherhood and common backgrounds, and given Lewis's status as national figure and territorial governor, Russell would have paid Lewis every possible courtesy. This was particularly true because the former brother officer who landed at the Bluffs was a sick man. As Russell would report in letters, a statement, and undoubtedly countless conversations, Lewis arrived in a "state of derangement," having already tried to kill himself twice. According to Russell, the primary cause of his disturbed state was his excessive drinking. Russell placed Lewis under close watch, provided medical attention, and was relieved when Lewis seemed to recover. On 29 September he saw him off with an escort for Nashville.

When Russell learned of Lewis's death he promptly sought the details and wrote letters to Lewis's friends relating what he knew. One of those friends was William Clark. The letters to Clark apparently have not survived, but part of their content is cited in a letter that Clark wrote his brother Jonathan on 26 November 1809 from Fincastle, where Russell's letters had caught up with him. "I have just receved letters from Capt. Russell who Commands at the Chickasaw Bluffs," wrote Clark, "that Govr. Lewis was there detained by him 15 days in a State of Derangement most of the time and that he had attempted to kill himself before he got there _ . . . Capt. rusell Sais he made his will at the Bluffs and left Wm. Merrewether & myself Execeters and derected that I Should dispose of his papers &c. as I wished _"[16] (See Document 7.)

In two letters to Jefferson dated 4 and 31 January 1810 and in a statement dated 26 November 1811 Russell provided crucial information about Lewis's state of mind while at the fort. Murder theorists often ignore the January letters and instead cite only the November 1811 statement, pointing to its two-year gap after Lewis's death to question its validity and motive, even going so far so to accuse Russell of being a conspirator in Lewis's death. Such a charge is completely unsupported by any documentation. In his 4 January 1810 letter to Jefferson, Russell related that Lewis's "situation" was such that it "rendered it necessary that he should be stoped until he would recover." In about six days he was "perfectly restored" but stayed at the fort another eight or nine days waiting to learn if Russell would receive permission to also go to Washington in regard to his own contested bills. In one of those seemingly small matters that loom large after events unfold, Russell was refused permission to leave his post at that time, and Lewis headed east with Major James Neelly. Russell clearly lamented the governor's death and believed he had done what he could. "As an individual I verry much regret the untimely ~~loss~~ death of Governor Lewis whose loss will be great to his country & severely felt by his friends," he wrote Jefferson.

"When he left this [place] I felt much satisfaction for indeed I thot I had been the means of preserving the life of one valuable man, and as it has turn'd out I shall have the conselation that I discharged those obligations towards him that man is bound to do his fellow."[17]

Russell's 4 January letter lacked details regarding Lewis's time at Fort Pickering. Apparently believing a fuller explanation of the explorer's stay there was desired, if not required, he provided more details in his 31 January 1810 letter to Jefferson:

> The fact in which you may yet be ignorant of [is] that his [Lewis's] un timely death may be attributed Solely to the free use he made of liquor which he acknowledged very candidly to me after he recovered & expressed a firm determination never to drink any more Spirits or use Snuff again both of which I deprived him of for Several days & confined him to Claret & a little white wine. But after leaving this place by some means or other his resolution left him and this agt. [Neelly] being extremely fond of liquor, instead of preventing the Govr. from drinking or puting him under any restraint, advised him to it & from every thing I can learn gave the man every chance to seek an opportunity to destroy himself. And from the statement of Grinders wife where he killed himself I cannot help believing that Purney [Pernier] was rather aiding & abeting in the murder than otherwise.[18]

Russell understandably sought to reassure Jefferson that he had taken every step possible to protect Lewis from destroying himself. He had heard that Neelly and Pernier had allowed—if not encouraged—Lewis to again drink to excess, with the consequence that he again became suicidal. How fair these charges against Neelly and Pernier were probably will never be known. Russell had learned details of Lewis's last days, including statements made by Priscilla Grinder, that apparently did not make it into published reports. From them he seemed to conclude that Neelly and Pernier did not watch over Lewis and protect him from himself as they should have, and he was incensed. His use of the word "murder" means self-murder and refers to Pernier's allowing Lewis to indulge his excesses and acquire the means to kill himself.[19]

In 1810 Russell traveled east himself to deal with his protested government bills. He was still in the East more than a year later, for in November 1811, while in Fredericktown (now Frederick), Maryland, he provided another statement regarding Lewis's death. (What took

Russell to Fredericktown that fall is not known, though he may have been attending the court-martial of James Wilkinson, a wily schemer who is also a suspect in some murder theories, though there is no proof against him.) On 26 November, Colonel Jonathan Williams, a fellow member, with Lewis, of the American Philosophical Society and the first superintendent of the U.S. Military Academy at West Point, received this statement from Russell concerning Lewis's death. Whether Russell was drawing from memory or working with notes and letters cannot be known. Nor can it be known why the statement was given. Perhaps it was provided for the army's records or in relation to some investigation. Perhaps it was made to satisfy the curiosity of Williams and other associates of Lewis's. Whatever the reason, it is an important statement and is quite consistent with the facts stated in Russell's letters to Jefferson of January 1810.[20] This statement is sometimes maligned by murder supporters. Its provenance and authenticity have been questioned, but there is no valid reason to doubt either. The document is clearly a clerical copy of the original that Williams retained for his personal papers. The only writing in Williams's hand is his signature verifying where and when the statement was taken.

In the statement, Russell reviewed Lewis's arrival at Fort Pickering in a "state of mental derangement, which appeared to have been produced as much by indisposition as other causes." (See Document 9 for full text.) Russell did not say what the "other causes" might have been, but they were conceivably of both physical and mental origin. The "derangement" was so severe that "on discovering his situation, and learning from the Crew that he had made two attempts to Kill himself, in one of which he had nearly succeeded, [I] resolved at once to take possession of him and his papers, and detain them there untill he recovered, or some friend might arrive in whose hands he could depart in Safety." It took Lewis "about five days" under continuous care before "all symptoms of derangement disappeared and he was completely in his senses and thus continued for ten or twelve days." But two weeks had not been sufficient to achieve a true recovery. Only days after setting off overland in the company of Chickasaw Indian agent James Neelly, an interpreter, Chickasaw chiefs, and servants, Lewis suffered a relapse. "By much severe depletion during his illness he had been considerably reduced and debilitated, from which he had not entirely recovered when he set off," Russell recalled, "and the weather in that Country being yet excessively hot and the exercise of traveling too Severe for him; in three or four days he was again affected with the same mental disease." Russell and the post doctor had been able to take charge of Lewis and help him at the Bluffs, but this unfortunately was not the case on the trail. "He had no person with him who could manage or controul him in his pro-pensities," Russell reported, "and he daily grew worse untill he arrived at the house of a Mr. Grinder . . . where in the apprehension of being destroyed by enemies which had no existence but in his wild immagina-tion, he destroyed himself, in the most Cool desperate and Barbarian-like manner, having been left in the house intirely to himself."[21]

Why was he by himself? Neelly and some Indians had stayed back at their camp of the night before to search for two horses that had roamed. Lewis went ahead with the servants and baggage horses to the first place owned by white people, where he was to wait for Neelly. As Russell explained, when Lewis arrived at Grinder's Stand, he

> refreshed himself with a little meal & drink [and] went to bed in a cabin by himself and ordered the Servants to go to the Stables and take care of the Horses, least they might loose some that night; some time in the night he got his pistols which he loaded, after every body had retired in a Seperate Building and dis-charged one against his forehead without much effect—the ball not penetrating the Skull but only making a furrow over it. He then discharged the other against his breast where the ball en-tered and passing downward thro' his body came out low down near his back bone. After Some time he got up and went to the house where Mrs. Grinder and her children were lying and asked for water, but her husband being absent and having heard the report of the pistols She was greatly allarmed and made him no answer. He then in returning got his razors from a port folio which happened to contain them and Seting up in his bed was found about day light, by one of the Servants, buisily engaged in cuting himself from head to foot. He again beged for water, which was given him and so soon as he drank, he lay down and died with the declaration to the Boy that he had Killed himself to deprive his enemies of the pleasure and honor of doing it.

Russell concluded his statement by saying how saddened everyone was by his death. "His death was greatly leamented," he said. "And that a fame so dearly earned as his Should finally be Clouded by Such an act of desperation was to his friends still greater Cause of regret."[22]

If murder theorists question Gilbert Russell's actions and information, they absolutely ridicule Priscilla Grinder's account. She and her husband are most often portrayed as the villains in Lewis's death. Over the years, her story found its way into print and oral tradition. The pro-murder group criticizes both her actions and her account of events. Over the years her story changed slightly. Some of the details not reported by Neelly in his letter to Jefferson were mentioned in Captain John Brahan's letter to the president, in Russell's statement, in Alexander Wilson's account, and in interviews many years later of the slave girl Malinda. All of them deserve close reading, but especially the accounts that are closest to the event. There might have been a certain amount of embellishment by Mrs. Grinder in her repeated telling of the sad events. This is certainly true for the account she told some thirty years later to an unnamed Arkansas schoolteacher whose version of Grinder's recollection appeared in newspapers in the mid-1840s. These differences have helped make Priscilla Grinder the focus of suspicion and ridicule by murder supporters. But that is the way of human memory, and her accounts, given at the time and in later years, always remained consistent in their main points. Much is made of the later rumors that her husband, Robert, murdered Lewis and that she was covering for him. The Grinders figure in the scenario that has Robert Grinder acting in concert with bandits who robbed and killed Lewis. And then there is the rumor that an outlaw named Thomas Runions murdered Lewis, shooting him in the back while Lewis was out on a walk. The connection? Runions later married into the Grinder family. According to this line of thinking, the Grinders protected themselves and their ill-gotten gains by claiming Lewis's death was a suicide. By the same token, they protected the reputation of their inn, the local area, and the trace. Such theories simply do not stand up to scrutiny.

James Neelly's account is closely connected to Priscilla Grinder's. He got the news of what happened at the inn from her and from Pernier, but he had also observed Lewis for almost a month before the latter's death. First at Fort Pickering and then on the trail until just a day away from Grinder's Stand, Neelly was with Lewis daily. The Indian agent has been criticized for not remaining with the explorer instead of going off in search of two strayed horses. But it was reported that Lewis asked him to remain behind. Not only was Neelly familiar with the area but if the journals and accounts were on those horses, then Neelly was providing an important service for Lewis, one Lewis would not have wanted to entrust to the servants. If he lost his journals and papers Lewis would count himself ruined. And in Lewis's agitated state, perhaps Neelly believed that getting him to an inn rather than allowing him to look for the horses was deemed the wisest course. Because of these actions, Neelly has been enmeshed in the conspiracy theorists' tales of being part of a plan to kill Lewis. But it is extremely unlikely that he was an assassin or a robber. All evidence indicates that he and Lewis met by chance at Fort Pickering, and since he was going the same way as Lewis, he simply agreed to accompany him. Neelly might have believed that he could stop the governor from engaging in certain behavior. Perhaps Lewis drank despite Neelly's efforts to stop him. Or perhaps Neelly, with his own reported weakness for the bottle, readily drank with Lewis, as Russell charged. It is inferred from Russell's statement that Lewis asked either Neelly or Pernier for his gunpowder, which had apparently been kept from him. Was this done out of fear that the governor would shoot himself or someone else in his derangement?

Neelly was among the first to take up pen and write of the tragedy to Jefferson. A week after Lewis's death, he provided the former president with the details: "It is with extreme pain that I have to inform you of the death of His Excellency Meriwether Lewis . . . who died on the morning of the 11th Instant and I am sorry to say by suicide." He recounted Lewis's reasons for changing his route eastward, his appearing "deranged in mind" while on the trail, and the sad facts as given to him by Priscilla Grinder and John Pernier.[23]

It must also be noted that the Neelly family was an established, respectable family in that region of Tennessee.[24] James Neelly might have been going to Nashville on business, but he was also going home for a visit. The Indian agent was not some shadowy drifter looking for a mark. He was a major in the Tennessee militia, a federal official, and someone known in the area. According to his statements, Neelly stood ready to help in any way he could regarding the tragedy. He reported that he retained some of Lewis's possessions until they could be safely delivered to the family and as security for a debt he believed he was owed by Lewis's estate. Russell disagreed with such a claim, but he did not know what expenses Neelly might have incurred in assisting Lewis. And some of Lewis's effects were indeed eventually returned to his family. To accuse Neelly, or even suspect him, of foul play requires complete rejection of the established facts of the case from a variety of sources.

What of John Pernier? His name appears as the suspect in Lewis and

Clark family lore and some murder theories. How likely is it that he would murder his master, change clothes with him, rob him, conspire with or threaten the Grinders into covering up the murder, and then fool everyone into believing that Lewis had killed himself? Pernier had been Lewis's servant since July 1807. There is neither reason nor proof to doubt his loyalty. He claimed that Lewis owed him more than two years in back wages, so he certainly had an interest in seeing Lewis safely to Washington and through his financial difficulties. Of even more importance is the questioning he undoubtedly underwent by Neelly, men in Nashville, and Jefferson. It is extremely unlikely that Pernier was capable of waiting for Neelly to arrive at Grinder's Stand in order to claim Lewis had killed himself and then successfully carry the charade through all the questioning he undoubtedly faced—at least without breaking under the strain. Everyone wanted answers to Lewis's suicide and Pernier was apparently able to satisfactorily provide them. If any of his interlocutors had harbored the least suspicion that Pernier had somehow dealt foully with his master, it would have been pursued. But he evidently stood up to the questioning and even came off as a sympathetic figure, loyal to Lewis and distraught by his death. He insisted on reporting on Lewis's death to Jefferson himself, another indication that Pernier had nothing to hide. Pernier used to work for the former president, so Jefferson knew him. The likelihood of his being able to deceive the Sage of Monticello, if he had murdered his protégé is very remote.[25] If Pernier had robbed Lewis, why not disappear down the Natchez Trace or flee to Nashville or Virginia, where he could have spent his ill-gotten gains? Instead, he is loaned money to complete his trip, pitied for his obviously distracted state, and trusted to report on Lewis's death to Jefferson.

The accounts presented by Neelly, Russell, and Brahan incorporate Pernier's recollection of Lewis's last hours with those of Priscilla Grinder. One new detail is contained in William Clark's 26 November letter to his brother Jonathan. Written on the same day that Pernier was with Jefferson at Monticello, Clark quoted the servant concerning Lewis's behavior. How the information came to Clark is not known. He either got it in a letter from one of his contacts in Tennessee or in a letter from Pernier himself. It is also a remote possibility that Pernier and Clark met on their mutual journeys eastward. They would have traveled part of the same route at approximately the same time. "His Servent reports," Clark wrote, "that 'on his way to nashvill, he [Lewis] would frequently 'Conceipt [conceive] that he herd me Comeing on, and Said that he was certain [I would] over take him, that I had herd of his Situation and would Come to his releaf.' "[26] (Clark was actually to the north, in Kentucky, when Lewis had these hallucinations and had no idea of his friend's distress.)

John Brahan, who identified himself as a good friend of Lewis's, wrote Jefferson on 18 October that Pernier was leaving the next morning for Monticello. He noted that Neelly had loaned Pernier some money, but fearing that would not be enough, Brahan had added to it. He was careful, however, not to give Pernier too much, being "fearful it might Cause him to drink as I discover he has a propensity at present." But Brahan did give him the benefit of the doubt, confessing that his drinking might be "from distress of mind at the death of the Governor."[27]

One final point should be made regarding Pernier. It has been said that Lewis's mother, Lucy Marks, accused him of her son's death. No contemporary source makes this claim. One must go to the claims of Meriwether Lewis Clark, William Clark Kennerly, and others to find such charges. (More on that later.) Had the Lewis family actually accused Pernier of murder, it probably would have devastated him. Surely such a charge would also have somehow appeared in Lewis family letters. Since Pernier had worked for Lewis since July 1807, the Lewis family would have had at least a passing acquaintance with him. By all accounts he was a loyal and faithful servant who strove to do his duty to the end by carrying word of his master's death all the way to Virginia.

After visiting Monticello, Pernier journeyed on to Washington. Jefferson had Pernier carry a letter to President Madison about Lewis's death in which he stated his sympathy for the servant's ordeal and situation. Once in Washington, Pernier stayed with John Christian Sueverman, a former servant of Jefferson's who operated a boardinghouse in the capital. Pernier was in bad health, was worried about being paid his back wages ($271.50 according to his calculation), and was "wretchedly poor and destitute." His apparent response to this despair was to kill himself with an overdose of laudanum on 29 April 1810. In August Jefferson noted Pernier's death in a letter to Lewis's kinsman and executor, William D. Meriwether. "You probably know the fate of Poor Pierney his [Lewis's] servant who lately followed his master's example."[28] Thus, Pernier was dead by May 1810, and the tales about his disappearing after Lewis's death or being accosted years later by Lewis family members are false.

The other important body of evidence resides with those who heard the news and contributed information about Lewis, including their personal knowledge of the explorer and why they believed he committed suicide. "I feel great distress at the premature death of the Governor," Captain Brahan confessed in his letter to Jefferson a week after the event. "[H]e was a very particular friend of mine, being intimately acquainted, and one for whom I had the Greatest Respect & Esteem."[29] Brahan talked to Pernier and Neelly about Lewis and voiced no suspicions regarding his friend's death. He reported some of the details of the death to Jefferson. How well he actually knew Lewis isn't known, but he accepted that Lewis was "Some what deranged in mind" while on the trace. He mentioned that one of the horses that had wandered off was Neelly's and one was Lewis's. Did Lewis see even greater debt and trouble for himself if the horse wasn't recovered? Brahan went on to report that Lewis suggested Neelly look for the horses while he continued on, to which the Indian agent agreed. Whether he agreed only if Lewis would take the servants with him is not known.[30]

William Clark's letters to his brother Jonathan are another important source for information on Meriwether Lewis. Clark's letters to Jonathan—his big brother, father figure, counselor, and friend—are an incredible archive providing the best known view of the personal William Clark, his opinions, hopes, dreams, fears, and more. They are a window to the man and his world. In his letters, Clark discussed with and confessed things to Jonathan that he did with no other known person. One of those subjects was Meriwether Lewis. His 26 November 1809 letter in which he passed along information from Gilbert Russell and John Pernier has already been quoted. Clark began worrying about his friend before either one of them left St. Louis in the late summer of 1809. He witnessed Lewis's difficulties and reaction to them. On 26 August he wrote Jonathan a letter saying that he had seen his friend off the day before. (In fact, though Clark didn't know it then, apparently Lewis did not leave St. Louis for another ten days.) Clark could not get Lewis and his troubled situation off his mind. "Govr. L. is r——d [ruined?] by Some of his Bills being protested for a Considerable Sum . . . all of which he has vouchrs for," Clark wrote. Lewis had expressed his distress to Clark "in Such terms as to Cause a Cempothy [sympathy] which is not yet off." William defended his friend's honor, declaring that there had never been "an honest er man in Louisiana nor one who had pureor motives than Govr. Lewis." But he could not help but worry about

Lewis and his mental state. "[I]f his mind had been at ease I Should have parted Cherefully," he confessed to Jonathan.[31] Part of Clark's own unease might have been caused by the fact that Lewis had turned over all his landed property to him and two other friends to be used to pay his debts. Did Clark think Lewis was determined to have his debts settled while absent from St. Louis, or did Clark wonder whether his friend ever intended to return? He refused to dwell on such a possibility. Although Lewis's situation was serious, he wrote Jonathan, "I think all will be right and he will return with flying Colours to this Country." But in the meantime, his friend's reputation was suffering and rumors were circulating. Clark discounted them and requested Jonathan to keep the information he imparted to himself, saying, "prey do not mention this about the Govr. excupt Some unfavourable or wrong Statement is made—I assure you that he has done nothing dis honourable, and all he has done will Come out to be much to his Credit—as I am fully purswaded." William Clark certainly wanted to believe that Lewis would be okay.[32]

William Clark started east with his family a month later, on 21 September. He needed to take care of some of his own business in Washington, and he and Julia looked forward to a visit with their families in Kentucky and Virginia. They arrived at Jonathan's place near Louisville on 12 October and left on 26 October. By the afternoon of 28 October they were passing through Shelbyville. While stopped there, William Clark read a newspaper report that Lewis had killed himself. He was stunned. That night, and periodically over the next month, he wrote Jonathan about this tragic event, relaying to him details he learned of Lewis's death and his own distress at the terrible news. It was an event that Clark rarely spoke of afterwards, but in those first weeks immediately after he learned of Lewis's death, he could hardly think of anything else. That night, he wrote Jonathan a letter in which he definitively stated that he believed Lewis, if he was indeed dead, had killed himself.

[W]hen at Shelbyville to day I Saw in a Frankfort paper called the Arguss a report published which givs me much Concern, it Says that Govr. Lewis killed himself by Cutting his Throat with a Knife, on his way between the Chickaw Saw Bluffs and nashville, I fear this report has too much truth, tho' hope it may have no foundation—my reasons for thinking it possible is founded on the letter which I recved from him at your house, in that letter he

Says he had Some intintion of going thro' by land & his only objection was his papers The Boats I Sent down with the pelteres [peltries], under the derections of Mr. James McFarlane must have over taken the Govr. between new madrid and the Chickasaw Bluffs, and if he was Still dis posed to go through, . . . is it not probable that he might have intrusted his papers to McFarlane who is a pertcular friend of his and on his way to the City of Washington? and Set out from the Bluffs with a view to pass thro' the most derect rout, which is by Nashville—I fear O! I fear the waight of his mind has over come him, what will be the Consequence? what will become of ~~my~~ his paprs? I must write to Genl. Robinson or Some friend about nashville to enquire about him, and Collect and Send me his papers, if he had any with him—I am quit[e] distressed about this report.[33]

This letter is sometimes actually used by murder supporters to buttress their contention that Clark did not believe Lewis had killed himself. (For the full text of the letter, see Document 5.) They interpret "it may have no foundation" to mean that Clark did not doubt Lewis was dead but doubted it was suicide.[34] The clear meaning, in context, is not that Clark doubted suicide but rather hoped the report that Lewis was dead was in error. What other meaning can the statement "I fear O! I fear the waight of his mind has over come him" have? Murder theorists generally discount or ignore this reaction by Clark or state that Clark was not at Grinder's Stand and therefore is not a credible source regarding Lewis's death. But Clark's reaction is credible and very important. Clark knew Lewis well. They had been together regularly over the last year—not to mention their previous association. Therefore, it is very significant that Clark's first reaction to the report that Lewis had killed himself was acceptance that his friend's disturbed mental state had caused him to commit suicide. To this should be added the letter, written at New Madrid, that Clark received from Lewis. Though, unfortunately, this letter has not survived, it apparently revealed a great deal concerning Lewis's mental state and intentions at a crisis point and was one of the major reasons Clark immediately believed the report that his friend had killed himself.

Two days later, writing from Lexington, Kentucky, Clark confessed to Jonathan that the news of Lewis's death weighed heavily on them. The day before, he had learned that Lewis was definitely dead, "which givs us much uneasiness." Clark wrote letters in an attempt to gather information about the tragedy and asked Jonathan to send him Lewis's letter from New Madrid. "I wish much to get the letter I receved of Govr. Lewis from N. madrid, which you Saw," he declared, "it will be of great service to me. prey Send it to Fincastle as Soon as possible."[35]

Taking the old Wilderness Road through the Cumberland Gap, the Clarks were in Bean Station, Tennessee, a little more than a week later. Clark was still reeling from the news of Lewis's death. "You have heard of that unfortunate end of Govr. Lewis," he wrote Jonathan. "I was in hopes of hearing more perticular[s] at this place, but have not __ . . . I am at a loss to know what to be at his death is a turble [terrible] Stroke to me, in every respect."[36] (See Document 6.)

Once the Clarks reached Julia's family in Fincastle, Virginia, the letters and reports about Lewis's death began catching up to William. There he received information about his partner in discovery from Gilbert Russell and John Pernier. He also heard from others, such as William Anderson of Nashville. Unfortunately, he didn't relay what their letters reported, and apparently none of this important correspondence has survived. But it moved Clark to comment about his friend, "pore fellow, what a number of Conjecturral reports we hear mostly unfavourable to him. I have to Contredict maney of them."[37] Clark's last comment is sometimes cited by murder proponents to support their contention of homicide. To me, it is clearly Clark's intent to defend his friend's honor and rebut some of the rumors circulating regarding charges of misconduct, imminent dismissal, and such. If William Clark, who knew Meriwether Lewis so well, had believed for one moment that the verdict of suicide was false and his good friend had not taken his own life, he would have demanded an investigation, and he certainly would have proclaimed it in his letters to Jonathan. Instead, he relays and comments on the news of his friend's death with sadness and resignation. Calling him a "pore fellow" certainly evokes an impression of pity rather than anger—a belief in suicide rather than murder.

These revealing letters to Jonathan are essentially William Clark's only known comments on Lewis's death. As previously stated, he afterward commented on it little. We have only scant references to his discussing Lewis's death with the Lewis family, with Jefferson, with Secretary of War William Eustis, or any others. If he ever entertained any belief in the possibility of murder, it undoubtedly would be found in documentary sources. As far as claims that Clark believed in later years that Lewis was murdered, there are no verifiable or reliable sources for such statements.

What of Thomas Jefferson? He clearly believed his protégé had killed himself. Strange to say, those who support murder seem to hold this belief against him. The pro-murder group believes that the Sage of Monticello betrayed or somehow dishonored Lewis and his memory by publicly acknowledging the verdict of suicide. From the moment he heard the news that his former private secretary had killed himself, Jefferson accepted it—and he certainly lamented it. He was in much the same position as William Clark; he had lived with Lewis and knew him well. He was able to base his acceptance of suicide on years of observation and knowledge of Lewis and the Lewis family. He wrote a biographical profile of Lewis four years after the explorer's death in which he noted that he "had from early life been subject to hypocondriac affections. It was a constitutional disposition in all the nearer branches of the family of his name, & more immediately inherited by him from his father."[38] Why should that be doubted? Jefferson was in a position to know the emotional ups and downs of the Lewis family. It certainly gave him no satisfaction to write that about Lewis and his family, but he wrote it because he knew it to be the truth.

Jefferson also observed that those "affections" had "not . . . been so strong as to give uneasiness to his family. While he lived with me in Washington, I observed at times sensible depressions of mind, but knowing their constitutional source, I estimated their course by what I had seen in the family."[39] But, say the murder theorists, if Jefferson had known Lewis was mentally unbalanced or really suffered any kind of mental disorder, he never would have chosen him for his long-dreamed-of western expedition. This is not the case. Jefferson believed he could gauge Lewis's mental ups and downs and despite his bouts with depression believed he was the best choice. "During his Western expedition the constant exertion which that required of all the faculties of body & mind, suspended these distressing affections; but after his establishment at St. Louis in sedentary occupations they returned upon him with redoubled vigor, and began seriously to alarm his friends. He was in a paroxysm of one of these when his affairs rendered it necessary for him to go to Washington," Jefferson wrote in his profile of Lewis. After reviewing Lewis's difficulties on his trip east—as reported to him by Russell, Neelly, Pernier, and Brahan—he then stated his opinion regarding Lewis's death: "[H]e did the deed that plunged his friends into affliction and deprived his country of one of her most valued citizens."[40] So writing, Jefferson believed he had given an accurate and truthful account of his late protégé and that posterity would declare that Lewis had not lived in vain.

Murder proponents have questioned the reliability of this biographical profile because it was written almost four years after Lewis's death. Saying that Jefferson had time to be influenced by events, especially politics, and abandon his protégé to the "stigma" of suicide in his desire to sweep the incident under the rug is unfair. Granted, Jefferson was no paragon of virtue, he did sometimes take the politically expedient course, and he could be something of a dilettante in his many and varied interests. But to accuse him of caring so little about Lewis that he rationalized his death and abandoned him to the charge of suicide in order to avoid any responsibility or scandal on his part is unfair. Jefferson believed Lewis killed himself, and he mourned the man and what might have been had he chosen to live.

If further proof is desired that Jefferson believed Lewis took his own life, a review of his correspondence provides it. The letters he wrote others regarding Lewis's death, which refer to Lewis in a vein of pity and sadness, clearly prove his belief in the verdict of suicide.[41] In his August 1810 letter to William Meriwether transmitting news of Pernier's death by suicide, he wrote that Pernier had "followed his master's example."[42] And then there is his response to Gilbert Russell's two letters of January 1810. Jefferson received Russell's 31 January letter with its details about Lewis on 16 April. Two days later he responded, expressing his thanks to all the friends who had helped the "unfortunate governor Lewis." He then left no doubt as to his opinion regarding the cause of his friend's death. "We have all to lament that a fame so dearly earned was clouded finally by such an act of desperation. He was much afflicted & habitually so with hypocondria. This was probably increased by the habit into which he had fallen & the painful reflections that would necessarily produce in a mind like his."[43] The "habit" was drinking heavily and perhaps even sinking into alcoholism. The consequences that alcohol can have in concert with depression are serious. Jefferson repeated the same beliefs more than three years later when he penned his biographical profile of Meriwether Lewis. If the Lewis family claimed Lewis's death was murder, would Jefferson be so insensitive to them as to bluntly state he believed it to be suicide if they did not? In that age of decorum and formality certainly not.

Letters written by others who knew Lewis echo the verdict of suicide. Not a whisper of murder or even suspicion has been found in contemporary accounts. Charles Willson Peale, artist, collector, and friend to both Jefferson and Lewis, reported to his son on 17 November 1809 that he had trouble believing the news, "but it comes now with so many circumstances as to force a credit to it. Governor Lewis has destroyed himself." Peale went on to explain that Lewis had lately been in bad health, "showed evident signs of mental disarrangement," and when embarrassed by protested bills the "mortification completed his despair."[44] The Lewis that Peale knew in 1803 and 1807 was quite different from the Lewis of 1809. It is understandable that Peale and others didn't want to believe the report, but when presented with details of Lewis's decline, they concluded he had done away with himself.

An important correspondent about Lewis's death is a member of his own family. William D. Meriwether was Lewis's cousin, guardian, friend, and executor of his estate. His correspondence with Clark, Jefferson, and others about the death and estate of his kinsman clearly indicates his belief—and thus that in general of the family—that Lewis killed himself. No whisper of murder ever appears in his letters. He wrote about Lewis's possessions and the expedition history. In a flash of anger at the government that reflects the blame he probably placed with it for Lewis's death, William Meriwether stated that he believed that Lewis and Clark had been "illy rewarded" for their service. With a perspective such as that he certainly would not have allowed Jefferson's comment to him that Pernier "followed his master's example" by committing suicide go unchallenged. He—and again, therefore, the family—obviously did not dispute the verdict of suicide.[45]

There were indications even before Meriwether Lewis's death that he was in a mental and emotional downward spiral and that his friends had great concern for him. Clark's August letter to Jonathan Clark has already been cited. Others also commented on Lewis's deteriorating state. Clement Penrose, a territorial official, came to the governor's defense against Frederick Bates's actions. He accused Bates of causing Lewis's "mental derangement" due to his "barbarous conduct" toward the governor in his attempt to "tear down" Lewis with "false and malicious" scandal and replace him as governor. Bates countered, adamantly, that he was not to blame for Lewis becoming "insane."[46]

An important piece of additional evidence supporting Lewis's mental decline is a tribute to him published in the 23 November 1809 edition of the *Missouri Gazette*. An unidentified person using the pseudonym "Z" wrote the letter on 19 November. "Z" was clearly a friend of Lewis's and greatly mourned his death. The tribute provides significant specifics about Lewis's mental state prior to leaving St. Louis. Z's ready acceptance that Lewis killed himself was based on his behavior that summer and further supports the verdict of suicide:

> To his country[']s foe he never could dissemble, – he warmly loved his friend and could forgive a private enemy. – He had a spirit to resent a wrong and a heart to forgive it. – But alas what a change he underwent at last – his mind enveloped in a cloud of miseries, distilled unhappily from a deranged immagination – some secret cause he might have had, yet none was evidently known to friends why thus he seemed so changed – he lost all confidence in man and thought himself in the midst of enemies – an ungentle proneness to doubt the views of those who loved to serve and see him happy, scar'd friendship away – his reason at last became dethroned, and he coolly did his own quietus make, with the cruel mean of pistols – he aim'd too well – the trigger drawn, ere a friendly hand could arrest his purpose, the horrid deed was done![47]

All other newspapers at the time also reported Lewis's death as a suicide. The major articles were those from the Nashville papers. The reports in the 20 October issues of the *Democratic Clarion* and an unidentified paper were reprinted in newspapers throughout the country. They related Neelly's and Pernier's accounts of Lewis's death and commented on the tragedy. After relating the details of the death, the *Clarion* reported that "he had been under the influence of a deranging malady for about six weeks—the cause of which is unknown, unless it was from a protest to a draft which he drew on the secretary at war, which he considered tantamount to a disgrace by government. In the death of governor Lewis the public behold the wreck of one of the noblest of men."[48]

The other paper reported:

> The governor had been in a bad state of health, but having recovered in some degree, set out from the Chickasaw Bluffs and in travelling from that to the Chickasaw nation, our informant says, he discovered that the governor appeared at times considerably

deranged, and on their arrival in the nation, having lost two horses, the governor proceeded on, and the gentleman detained with a view of hunting the horses. The governor went on to a Mr. Grinder's on the road, found no person at home but a woman: she observing something wild in his appearance, become frightened and left the house to sleep in another near it, and the two servants that was with him went to sleep in the stable. About three o'clock the woman says she heard the report of two pistols in the room where he lay, and immediately awaked the servants, who rushed into the house, but too late. He had shot himself in the head and just below the breast, and was in the act of cutting himself with a razor. The only words he uttered were, "It is done, my good servant give me some water," and expired in a few moments after.

It is impossible to form any correct conjecture what ever could have produced so horrid a determination in the mind of a man, whose respectability and talents were so pre-eminent as those of the deceased. . . . He gave directions some days previous to his committing the act, that if any accident should happen to him, his trunks should be sent on to the President of the United States: from which circumstance we concluded that from some unknown cause, he had been induced to commit the rash deed; he had been often heard to speak of drafts which had been protested by the secretary of war, and it is supposed this circumstance may have occasioned his uneasiness of mind.[49]

The two reports differ in some of the details, just as Priscilla Grinder's did upon repeated telling. Murder supporters regularly point to such inconsistencies as proof of lying and a cover-up. The more logical explanation is that, in the retelling by those involved and then the subsequent restatement by those who heard or read the reports, minor contradictions arose. But the basic facts remained consistent.

News was quickly dispatched to St. Louis. The 2 November issue of the *Missouri Gazette* announced Lewis's death. It stated that those with him "became much alarmed at the governors behavior, he appeared in a state of extreme mental debility, and before he could be prevented, discharged the contents of a brace of pistols in his head and breast, calling to his servant to give him a bason of water; he lived about two hours and died without much apparent pain." The *Gazette* then commented on

Lewis's health before leaving St. Louis. "The governor has been of late very much afflicted with fever, which never failed of depriving him of his reason, in this cause we may ascribe the fatal catastrophe!"[50]

Various reports were published in the ensuing months, often repeating the basic facts but sometimes adding new information or speculation as to the cause of Lewis's suicide. In April 1810 an editorial in the *Monthly Anthology and Boston Review* speculated that the "indifference of the publick, and the very small number of subscribers it [the expedition history] has obtained, operated strongly on his mind, and was one of the causes that led to his unfortunate death."[51] There might have been some truth in that report.

Ornithologist Alexander Wilson was another of Lewis's friends shocked by his death and the manner of it. In 1811 he journeyed south and visited Grinder's Stand to see where his friend had died and talk to witnesses about his last hours. Wilson's letter relating his visit and interview with Priscilla Grinder is one of the primary accounts of Lewis's death. About one and a half years had passed since Lewis's death and in Grinder's telling about what happened that night a few of the details differed from the 1809 accounts, and some were added. Murder proponents point to these inconsistencies as evidence of foul play. It is much more likely that in the months after the tragedy more facts, and perhaps some embellishment and confusion of facts, were related by Priscilla Grinder. There might be some exaggeration and some minor misstatements in what she told Wilson, but he certainly did not doubt her account, and we have no reason to do so today. Wilson recorded her memories of Lewis's erratic and alarming behavior, how he kept walking back and forth and talking to himself. When the servants entered the room after he'd shot himself, he begged them to finish the job and put him out of his misery, repeating, "I am no coward; but I am *so* strong, *so hard to die*." Wilson was also a poet, and he was moved to write a poem about Lewis's tragic departure from the world: "The anguish that his soul assailed, / The dark despair that round him flew, / . . . / Poor Reason perished in the storm / And Desperation triumphed here! / . . . / Pale Pity consecrates the spot, / Where poor lost LEWIS now lies low!" Such sentiments leave no doubt as to Wilson's conclusion of suicide and are a touching memorial to the explorer.[52]

The people around Lewis who left any kind of documentary record all believed he had killed himself. From those on the scene like Russell and Neely to Lewis's best friend Clark and mentor Jefferson the unanimous conclusion was suicide. If someone had known or suspected differently, enough people were involved that word of their doubts would have somehow made it into writing. The evidence overwhelmingly pointed to suicide. Facts were facts and events were events, sad and tragic as they were. In the days, months, and years following Lewis's death the verdict of suicide never wavered.

The 1809 verdict of suicide apparently went unquestioned for almost forty years. Then, in December 1843 Tennessee passed legislation to create a county named in honor of Meriwether Lewis. In 1848 five hundred dollars was authorized to build a monument atop the explorer's grave. Lewis was a hero, but he was a flawed hero. The committee was faced with the prevailing belief that he had committed the socially and morally reprehensible act of taking his own life. Or had he? Without citing any local evidence or even rumors, the committee made the statement that it was more probable Lewis had "died by the hands of an assassin." If new information supported the statement, such as the actions of the Grinders or the findings of a coroner's panel that might have investigated Lewis's death, it was not mentioned. Where did the evidence of murder come from?

It is possible that the son of William Clark and Lewis's namesake, Meriwether Lewis Clark, was the catalyst. In a letter to a Reverend James Cressey of Maury County, Tennessee, regarding the monument, M. Lewis Clark asked whether Cressey had ever heard the tale that Lewis had not killed himself but had been murdered and robbed by his servant. In that same letter, Clark wrote, "This is an important matter in connection with the erection of a monument to his memory, as it clearly removes from my mind, at least, the only stigma upon the fair name I have the honor to bear."[53] Significantly, M. Lewis Clark did not reference his father as the source or even as a supporter of this story. Did father and son ever discuss Lewis's death? If such a discussion did take place, there is no known record of it. And it would have been years later. Meriwether Lewis Clark turned nine months old on 10 October 1809. If they did discuss it and William Clark stated he suspected murder rather than suicide, such information undoubtedly would have been well known in the Clark family. Instead, M. Lewis Clark cited the "tale," without attribution, that Lewis's servant had murdered him. Clark went on to confess the relief and satisfaction that a statement from the committee supporting murder would bring him in removing the "stigma" from the name he proudly bore. Did the committee grasp at this story as a means of exonerating Lewis of the onus of suicide? And by doing so, did they believe they were also doing the monument, the new county, Tennessee, and even themselves a service?

Essentially the same story was reported in William Clark Kennerly's memoir, *Persimmon Hill*. As interesting and informative as the memoir is, it is also unreliable. Using memory as well as notes, stories, and diaries, Kennerly's daughter, Elizabeth Russell, wrote the narrative in the mid-twentieth century. The "memoir" confuses fact and fiction and serves as a testament to the fallibility of memory and tendency to romanticize the past. Kennerly was born in St. Louis in 1825, sixteen years after Lewis's death. Consequently, he could only have heard rumors and tradition about Lewis's death. By the time his memories of life in Saint Louis were recorded by his daughter, any amount of embellishment about his Uncle William's partner in discovery might have been added. Eminent Lewis and Clark scholar Donald Jackson noted another source for Kennerly's memories: novelist Eva Emery Dye. Some of Kennerly's stories are actually quotes or paraphrases from the pages of Dye's novel *The Conquest*, which was based on the expedition.[54] Given this source, it is quite possible that others claiming murder at the turn of the century, such as Lewis and Clark editor Elliott Coues, influenced Kennerly's "memories."

Kennerly focused on the murder-robbery theory, identifying the Grinders, unnamed Natchez Trace bandits, and Pernier as suspects. What was the source for his conjectures? M. Lewis Clark? Lewis family members? Coues? It wasn't his Uncle William. Kennerly had talked to people about Lewis's death, "always hoping the mystery might be solved," but Clark wasn't one of them. Kennerly confessed that "Uncle Clark never spoke of it to us, and we sensed his reluctance to probe an old wound and forbore questioning him."[55] The "old wound" of his friend's death was undoubtedly painful to William Clark, but certainly he would have welcomed an opportunity to air his views and defend his friend if he believed he had been murdered.

If later generations of the Clark family claimed foul play and murder, the stories put forth by Lewis family members, and the purported facts to support the stories, are often contradictory, implausible, and erroneous. These reports began appearing in Lewis family histories by the mid-nineteenth century, thus spreading and helping to entrench the tales of robbery and murder even further. The stories are generally based on negative "evidence": Someone like Lewis would not have committed suicide, so it had to be murder.[56]

Did the Clark and Lewis families' claims influence the monument committee in its finding for murder? The committee probably also reviewed local tradition and rumors regarding Lewis's death. An 1844 Arkansas schoolteacher's account that cast suspicion on Pernier might have been read by the members.[57] The account itself stated that Lewis had killed himself but also related strange and mysterious facts surrounding his death, including the assertion that Pernier was wearing Lewis's clothes and that Pernier later cut his own throat. The teacher's account clearly seems to be part of the body of evidence that helped form local tradition and was used by later researchers and writers. But that "evidence" did not support murder in 1809 or a century later, and it does not support it today. Did the psychological and social discomfort of naming a county and erecting a monument to someone—no matter how deserving—who had taken his own life in the "most cool desparate and Barbarian-like manner"[58] encourage the committee members, consciously or subconsciously, to lean toward murder, using any kind of information to support that finding that they could?

The reasons for such unsupported statements and beliefs by family members and others are easily deduced. No one wanted to believe that this American hero had taken his own life. People didn't want to believe it in 1843 when Lewis County was created nor in 1848 when the monument was erected. And they certainly didn't want to believe it as the expedition's centennial approached and more histories and novels about the journey appeared. It was more desirable to believe that Lewis fell victim to robbers, that he was killed for his money or for the map of a secret gold mine he had discovered on the expedition, or that he knew too much about certain government officials and intrigues. Assassination was a much more honorable ending.

These rumors made the rounds for the last half of the nineteenth century. No proof was ever produced, and records that would help document the claims invariably went missing. But the rumors persisted and in the closing years of the century they ascended to a national stage. A growing number of murder theorists wrote that it was not "dark despair" that overcame the explorer that October night in the Tennessee woods, but rather foul play.

The first argument that disseminated this claim nationally can be dated to 1893 and the publication of Elliott Coues's edition of the history of the Lewis and Clark Expedition. While Coues admitted conclusive evidence was lacking, homicide was a view that the opinionated Coues embraced and avidly promoted. In his supplement to Jefferson's biography of Lewis, Coues relied on an article by a Tennessee lawyer named James D. Park as his primary source.[59] Coues proclaimed that Park's article finally revealed the truth regarding the great explorer's death. To a skeptical audience the evidence seems far from convincing, but Coues readily embraced Park's argument, contradictions and all.

Park's article appeared in the 6 September 1891 *Nashville American*. He apparently was the first person to try to document specific local rumor to prove Lewis was murdered, and he depended on second- and thirdhand reports to build his case. His primary source was a seventy-seven-year-old local resident named Christina B. Anthony. Park described her as a "bright, active, intelligent old lady." Anthony's primary source was another local woman named Polly Spencer, who was said to have been a servant of the Grinders and a witness to Lewis's death. Anthony heard Polly's story in the 1830s. It was a story Polly told often, according to Anthony, before her death about 1850. Her account, as remembered by Anthony and recorded by Park, differed in several significant respects from that reported at the time of Lewis's death. Most significant was Polly's recollection that Lewis was shot only once, soon after supper, and was dead when they reached him. According to her, Robert Grinder was promptly suspected of shooting and robbing Lewis, because only twenty-five cents was found in the governor's possession following his death. Grinder, who was of "Indian blood," fled, was captured, and tried for murder, but was released because of lack of evidence. After his release, the formerly poor Grinder moved to western Tennessee, where he reportedly "bought a number of slaves and a farm, and seemed to have plenty of money."[60]

Anthony supported this version of the story, remembering that local people always believed Grinder killed Lewis and took his money and that she had never heard the suicide theory until Park mentioned it. She provided Park with the names of two people a little older than herself who she thought would be able to give him more details about the murder. However, Park found it "inconvenient" to follow up these promising leads. He did report interviewing other local people, who, like Anthony, remembered the general consensus at the time was that Grinder had observed that Lewis was a man of distinction and wealth who was traveling almost alone. Believing that Lewis probably carried a lot of money with him, Grinder killed him. After all, Park concluded, Lewis was too young, successful, admired, brave, conscientious, and famous to "cowardly sneak out of the world by the back way, a self-murderer." It was inconceivable that he would do such a thing. The whole idea of suicide was invented to cover up the crimes of murder and robbery.[61]

There are several problems with Park's conclusions, chief among them being the acceptance of decades-old stories as fact and a subsequent leap of faith. Park clearly did not want to believe that Lewis killed himself. Documents from Lewis's own records prove that he was not carrying enough money, especially in cash, to allow Grinder to buy slaves and a farm and have money to spare.[62] Although it is possible that cash went missing after his death, there was some listed in the inventory of his effects—much more than twenty-five cents. It is established fact that Lewis borrowed money from Gilbert Russell; sent his land grant, a reward from the expedition, to New Orleans to be sold; and was trying to collect debts he was owed—all to stave off complete financial collapse and to meet anticipated traveling expenses.

It is also strange that, as sensational an event as Lewis's death was, Anthony claimed never to have heard that it had been called a suicide. In hearing the story from Polly Spencer, it would logically follow that she would have recalled that suicide was officially accepted, even though murder was suspected. And what about the purported coroner's jury that subsequent writers frequently cite? Spencer would have known about this. The whole affair was the talk of the neighborhood.

Polly's story as reported, and accepted, by Park also incorporated a flawed timeline. If indeed Robert Grinder had killed Lewis, fled, was caught, tried, released, and then moved away, what was he doing at the stand in May 1811 when Alexander Wilson visited? Wilson stated that Grinder showed him Lewis's grave and that he agreed to care for his friend's final resting place.[63] Indeed, public records verify, contrary to Spencer's and Anthony's stories, that the Grinders did not move to west Tennessee and were respected residents of Hickman County for many years.

This brings us to another matter: Park's reliance on Anthony. He listed her and two other sources she gave him (the persons he found "inconvenient" to visit) by name and age. Other informants remain anonymous. A simple analysis of Anthony's age and the ages of the other two sources Park cited as corroborating her story reveals that there was plenty of time for local rumor to embellish the story. If their ages as listed by Park at the time of his visit with Anthony in 1889 are to be believed, then Anthony was born about 1812, her brother Jason Boshears about 1809, and Sallie Barham Sims about 1807. Given that his star source wasn't born until some three years after Lewis's death and the others were approximately newborn and two years old, the reliability of Anthony's testimony grows even more questionable. A decade or more would have passed after Lewis's death before these sources would have been old enough to clearly remember what locals recalled about that night and any subsequent events. Spencer recounted the events to Anthony some twenty to forty years after they occurred; and it was some forty to sixty years since Anthony had heard the story from her. Local records do not support her (and others') statement of an arrest and trial for murder. Records for this period are claimed to be missing—further proof, it's said, of a cover-up by officials or Grinder supporters. Others have disputed the charge of missing records. And some have said that such documents were not maintained by the courts until several years afterwards and would therefore not be found in the county records. In a word, the records support Grinder's innocence, not his guilt.

Park's final argument is that Lewis must have been murdered because he would not have committed suicide. Such a claim is groundless. Given certain circumstances, anyone is capable of suicide. Many seemingly sane, healthy, and even happy individuals have taken their own lives. Lewis faced severe difficulties on a number of fronts, and all contemporary sources pronounced it suicide. Wishful thinking and a desire to clear a hero's name from the "stigma" of suicide cannot change that.

With Park's article as the foundation of his argument for murder, Elliott Coues embraced all findings casting doubt on suicide and thanked Park for "undertaking to clear so great a name from so grave an imputation."[64] In addition to Park's article, Coues used a selection of contemporary reports, subsequent local tradition, and his own desire to exonerate Lewis of the charge of self-destruction. Coues admitted that he could not prove the explorer's death to be murder but insisted that it was unfair to accuse him of suicide. Therefore, "until other evidence is forthcoming the victim of untimely fate should be given the full benefit of the doubt, that no stigma may rest on his illustrious name."[65]

Coues's history signaled a renewed national interest in the Lewis and Clark adventure. The end of an era of American westward expansion and the centennial of the expedition served as historic milestones in the minds of Americans. Other works about the expedition and its members, historical and fictional, followed Coues's over subsequent decades. Whether histories, biographies, novels, or articles, the works often addressed Lewis's death, thus continuing to stir the growing murder-versus-suicide debate. Some were quite influential in moving public opinion toward the belief that Lewis's death was a Judas-like scene of robbery, intrigue, and betrayal, resulting in murder. All the works that support murder that I have reviewed repeat family tradition and rumor, often ignoring important facts and references or twisting those they do cite.

In 1904 Tennesseean William Webster used unreliable local information and rumor to present a rather fantastic tale of multiple murder, theorizing that after Lewis was murdered by Robert Grinder, his "Indian guide and Spanish body servant . . . were also shot and hidden, in order to create the impression that they committed the murder, and ran away, but they were never found or arrested." Webster insisted that it was established fact that Grinder was arrested and charged with the murder. He also cited a conversation with the purported post rider, Robert O. Smith, who claimed he had found Lewis's body by the side of the road. There is serious doubt that Smith could have been that rider, if there was a rider at all. In defending Lewis, Webster proclaimed that Lewis went overland from the Mississippi because that was the fastest route and that, determined as he was to reach Washington, he would not have killed himself. To accuse Lewis of suicide, Webster said, was an "injustice" to one of the "greatest Anglo-Saxons that ever lived."[66]

And so went the arguments for and proof of murder, one after another. Park and Webster were important sources for Lewis and Clark authors such as Olin Wheeler, John Bakeless, Vardis Fisher, Richard Dillon, and others who argued for murder.[67] Rumor, negative evidence, and flawed logic all became the bases of their cases. For instance, Richard Dillon, in his *Meriwether Lewis: A Biography*, described Lewis as the epitome of the "anti-suicide type," who was a "fighter, not a quitter," and "one of the most positive personalities in American history." His conclusion: "Meriwether Lewis has not been proven guilty of self-destruction . . . therefore, let him be found NOT GUILTY of the charge—the crime of suicide."[68] Vardis Fisher's *Suicide or Murder? The Strange Death of Governor Meriwether Lewis* is frequently cited by murder theorists. But for those who disagree with Fisher, his use of facts and tradition is questionable. Donald Jackson characterized Fisher as a

"detective following a very cold trail," who relied on oral tradition, negative evidence, and the manipulation of facts in building a case for homicide. Fisher was basically a storyteller, Jackson said, and the facts kept
getting in the way of the story he wanted to tell.[69]

It was probably inevitable that in a desire to actually see and test any
possible evidence, modern science would be applied. It was in the early
1990s that law professor and self-proclaimed forensic sleuth James
Starrs proposed that the remains under the Lewis monument be exhumed and tested forensically in an attempt to answer the question of
murder or suicide. Starrs was in the news often during that period for his
involvement in digging up famous people who had met a mysterious or
disputatious end. His public statements and presentations made it clear
that in Meriwether Lewis's case he supported the murder theory. In
1996 the movement to exhume Lewis's remains (if the remains under
the monument are indeed those of Lewis) might have reached its zenith,
when Starrs organized a two-day coroner's inquest at Hohenwald, Tennessee, into Lewis's death. It resulted in a recommendation for exhumation so that appropriate tests could be performed on the remains.[70] It is
debatable how useful such tests might be. The final decision lies with the
National Park Service because Lewis's grave lies inside the boundaries
of the Natchez Trace National Parkway. As of 2005 permission for exhumation had not been granted.

Another witness at the Hohenwald inquest was my friend John
Guice. He repeated many of the arguments questioning the reliability of
the people and reports concerning Lewis's death. Guice echoed Bakeless's and Dillon's charges that Priscilla Grinder, a woman living on
the frontier, would not have been "timid" regarding Lewis's behavior.
Therefore, in concocting her story, Mrs. Grinder had something to
hide. Yet, a woman alone with children at a wayside inn faced with a
deranged stranger would seem to have good reason to be frightened.
Regarding Jefferson's and Clark's ready acceptance of suicide, Guice
stated that both men rationalized the claim of suicide—the former because he wanted to avoid a messy political situation and the panic on the
frontier that Lewis's murder would have caused and the latter because
he was powerless to do anything about it.[71]

Guice's 2002 article, "Moonlight and Meriwether Lewis," intro-
duced the darkness of the night as an important piece of evidence in a
case for murder. Guice argued that, on the night of 10 October 1809, a
barely visible moon would have rendered the night too dark for Mrs.

Grinder to see what she claimed to see regarding Lewis, thus rendering her account unreliable. Guice noted that her account made no mention of lanterns, candles, a fire, or any other light source being used. Starlight, he said, would have been insufficient to illuminate the scene.[72]

Many details regarding that night were not recorded. Such common details as the use of candles or lanterns are especially unlikely to be mentioned. They would be taken for granted. One needs only to read letters and diaries to realize how much is *not* reported. The expedition journals of Lewis and Clark provide ample examples of this. It is certainly possible, if not probable, that Lewis was using some kind of light in his room—a candle, a lantern, or a fire—to provide illumination; and if so, it is certainly possible that by such a source Mrs. Grinder was able to see Lewis pacing back and forth in his room and stumbling around between the cabins. The fact that such details were not recorded should not be used against witnesses' testimony. In addition, it is possible that the clearing around the cabin area allowed enough natural light, such as starlight, for Mrs. Grinder to see the dreadful scene unfolding before her.

On the other side of the debate regarding Lewis's death are, of course, those who believe the explorer *did* take his own life. Those who believe Lewis killed himself hold to that position not because of any sense of pleasure or satisfaction derived from it. On the contrary, the great explorer's death is as saddening and regrettable to them as to those who believe he was murdered. But they believe in the verdict of suicide because that is where an objective study of the facts leads them. It wasn't until claims of murder gained national prominence that they believed it necessary to defend the original verdict of suicide. And they believe the evidence convincingly points to suicide.

The first major argument in defense of the verdict of suicide was made by a Tennessean from the Lewis County neighborhood. John H. Moore wrote an article that appeared in 1904.[73] Moore presented evidence contradicting Park's and Webster's claims that local residents believed Lewis was murdered. Citing a long association with the Grinder family and a personal interview done about 1885 with the by-then-elderly former slave Malinda, who witnessed the events of that night, Moore presented a local perspective concerning Lewis's death quite different from that put forth by murder proponents. He also had a family connection to the debate. His father, Samuel Moore, was a member of the Lewis Monument Committee.

When John Moore interviewed Malinda about her memories of that night, he noted that her recollection was amazingly similar to the account Priscilla Grinder had related to Alexander Wilson in 1811. Malinda was about twelve in 1809, and the other family slave, Pete, was about thirteen. They were there with Priscilla Grinder and her children while Robert Grinder was at their Swan Creek farm getting in the crop. Malinda recalled that the "Governor" acted very agitated, walking around and talking to himself, saying, "They have told lies on me and want to ruin me." She remembered that the two servants with Lewis were afraid to stay in the house with him because he'd been acting strangely for two or three days, and they chose to sleep in the barn. The children fell asleep but not Mrs. Grinder. Worried about Lewis and his behavior, she sat up all night. Just before daybreak two shots sounded. As the governor crawled about and writhed in pain on the floor, Pernier came to the house. Together—Mrs. Grinder, the children, and Pernier—they went to the cabin where Lewis lay. Mrs. Grinder asked Lewis why he had shot himself, and he responded that if he hadn't done it someone else would have. Then he repeated, "They are telling lies and trying to ruin me." He drank the water given him but threw it up. He was in great pain and lingered until about noon.[74]

Some of the details in Malinda's story as recorded by Moore varied from the initial reports, but otherwise essentially agreed with Priscilla Grinder's account. Moore noted that the wife of the Grinders' son, Captain Robert Grinder, Jr., substantiated Malinda's story.[75] How reliable are Malinda's and the daughter-in-law's recollections in support of suicide? That has been subject to debate. It should be noted that these stories are also cited as sources by murder theorists. And some parts of the stories are hard to credit, involving gold, jewels, and Pernier's suicide.

As for James Park and his article, Moore credited it as putting into wide circulation the claim that Robert Grinder had killed Lewis and robbed him. Moore believed Park was "imposed upon by a garrulous and sensational old woman"—Christina Anthony.[76] Moore noted that she had not lived in the immediate area her whole life and that she had a bone to pick with the Grinders because one of her daughters had eloped with a Grinder, a grudge she still held many years later. In short, she was trying to exact revenge on the Grinder family and seized the opportunity to accuse their ancestor of the murder and robbery of Meriwether Lewis. To contradict malicious rumors about the Grinders, Moore cited a history of Hickman County (Grinder's Stand was in Hickman County prior to the creation of Lewis County) and an 1879 statement by Malinda about that night. He also cited records showing that the Grinders moved back to the Duck River area where they had previously lived and were respectable citizens in Hickman County for the rest of the century.[77]

Moore also sought to validate James Neelly's actions in leaving Lewis to look for the two strayed horses. What if those horses carried the packs containing Lewis's official papers and the expedition journals? One can imagine Lewis's distress at losing his papers or even a horse. Someone teetering on the edge of financial collapse could not easily dismiss the loss of a horse. And the possibility of losing the expedition journals and papers might well have been too much to bear. For Lewis, everything depended on those documents. It was imperative they be recovered. Who better to do so than Neelly, who knew the area and its people? A number of Neellys lived in this part of Tennessee. Hence, Lewis asked Neelly to look for the horses, and Neelly responded in good faith. He did, in fact, recover one of the horses. Whether it was carrying Lewis's papers is not known. There is no mention of papers being with Lewis the night of his death.[78]

Moore also made the point that the Lewis Monument Committee cited M. Lewis Clark rather than local evidence of Lewis's "murder." Moore reported he knew of no local stories prior to the 1840s saying that Lewis had been murdered. M. Lewis Clark's letter, most likely written in 1848, planted the murder seed, Moore believed, and now rumor and conjecture as to who might have been a party to Lewis's murder was afoot. Moore stated that his whole life had been spent in the area, and in all those years, from about 1840 to 1900, among the many, many people he had talked with, he had found few who believed Lewis had been murdered. Longtime and respected citizens of the area, Moore stated, agreed with him.[79] Logic and understanding are not part of madness's formula. Moore stated it very well: "Insanity furnishes its own motives." The years had worn Lewis down physically, mentally, and emotionally, and the "cord broke which had been stretched so tensely for years; his mind gave way; and, with his own pistol, he ended his troubles and his life."[80]

Moore's reasoned and knowledgeable argument in support of suicide was not widely circulated. But the murder theories of Coues, Wheeler, Bakeless, Fisher, and others were. It would be more than fifty years after the appearance of Moore's article before another important work appeared in defense of the verdict of suicide. In 1956 Dawson Phelps published "The Tragic Death of Meriwether Lewis" in the *William and Mary Quarterly*. Phelps argued convincingly for Lewis's killing himself. He cited the problems regarding the murder contentions, demonstrating how it wasn't possible for some of them to be true. Phelps then reviewed Lewis's troubled postexpedition life and quoted from contemporary sources, citing their consistency and reliability. Men like Gilbert Russell and James Neelly were respected and responsible military and government officials, Phelps noted. And John Pernier was not a suspect. There is no hint of foul play in their actions. Murder theorists have criticized Phelps for his statement that the Natchez Trace was safe for travelers in 1809, by which he discounted another theory that Lewis was murdered and robbed by unidentified outlaws. His critics claim that as the National Park Service historian for the Natchez Trace Parkway, he wanted to protect the historic road's reputation. Some crime undoubtedly existed on the trace, but it was not a regular and serious problem and it was only years later that rumors began circulating that Lewis had been the victim of outlaws.

Phelps's conclusion was reasonable fifty years ago and it still is today. "In the absence of direct and pertinent contemporary evidence of the contrary, of which not a scintilla exists," he wrote, "the verdict of suicide must stand. . . . That nearly thirty years passed before the possibility of murder was raised is in itself evidence of a high order that the original verdict of suicide was correct. Nothing has been offered since that time which can seriously challenge the fact that Meriwether Lewis died by his own hand."[81]

Donald Jackson reached the same conclusion. Editor of the *Letters of the Lewis and Clark Expedition*, Jackson did not devote entire books or even articles to Lewis's death, but he did review the evidence and he read the growing body of work that argued both for and against suicide. Then he stated his opinion. His conclusion was that Lewis had almost certainly taken his own life.[82]

In 1986 Paul Russell Cutright published the article "Rest, Rest, Perturbed Spirit." Cutright believed that Lewis had committed suicide. He offered his argument using a three-step process: (1) a summary of the problems Lewis faced after the expedition; (2) the events surrounding his death; and (3) an appraisal of the controversy that occurred years after Lewis's death claiming he had been killed. Cutright listed the various factors that led to Lewis's breakdown and death. He reviewed the

Russell, Neelly, and Wilson accounts of Lewis's last days and death—all expressing complete belief that he had died by his own hand. Cutright also reviewed the rise of the murder theory and its many flaws. Murder proponents might be capable of ignoring or making light of Lewis's problems, Cutright observed, but Lewis certainly wasn't. His whole world was unraveling and he saw no escape except in death.[83]

If suicide is accepted as the reason for Lewis's death, then the act must be explained. There are a variety of medical theories, based on both Lewis's physical and mental health, that hypothesize the reason for his self-destruction. Not surprisingly, they have their supporters and detractors—even among those who support suicide.

Physically, the diagnoses focus on two causes, cerebral syphilis and malaria. In 1994 epidemiologist Reimert Ravenholt garnered nationwide attention for his theory that *neurosyphilis paresis*, or the last horrible stage of cerebral syphilis, caused Lewis to shoot himself. He went so far as to claim that Lewis acquired the sexually transmitted disease in August 1805 from a Shoshone woman. Many people, including medical professionals, question this. Was a Rocky Mountain tryst Lewis's undoing? It cannot be completely rejected, but Ravenholt's theory is generally discounted.[84] As for malaria, it is accepted by many that Lewis suffered from its debilitating effects. Thomas Danisi claimed that Lewis was driven to near insanity by the disease, especially by the pain it caused. In Lewis's case, the pain was concentrated in his head and torso. According to Danisi's line of reasoning, when he put the pistols to his head and body, Lewis was not trying to kill himself, he was desperately trying to make the pain stop. The explorer's reported slashing of his body with a razor was a continuation of this delirious and tragic self-surgery.[85] This theory is not widely accepted either. Instances of malaria in this degree of severity are rare, and some doctors argue that there is no evidence that Lewis suffered from a case so advanced that it would drive him to suicide.

Did a lethal combination of depression, alcohol, and drugs prove to be Meriwether Lewis's undoing? At the time, depression and alcohol were the causes given for his suicide. David Peck, author of *Or Perish in the Attempt: Wilderness Medicine in the Lewis & Clark Expedition*, favors depression combined with the use of alcohol and opium. Those together, he wrote, are a "lethal combination," citing a suicide rate as high as 15 percent for those suffering from severe depression.[86] Many medical professionals, scholars, and laypeople support this theory.

Three interesting studies delve into Lewis's mental state and suicide. In 1981 historian Howard Kushner addressed Lewis's death using a psychoanalytical approach. He applied the method to Lewis's life, especially his postexpedition life, and accounts of his death and formed the hypothesis that Lewis suffered from a psychological disorder known as incomplete mourning.[87] It can occur when the mourning process is interrupted or some seed of guilt or resentment toward the deceased remains and festers. Repercussions can be depression, excessive risk taking, and self-punishment, which can lead to suicidal tendencies. Did the death of Lewis's father and stepfather, a loving but sometimes strained relationship with his mother, his unfilled desire to find a wife, his difficulty in maintaining personal relationships, and professional disappointments ultimately bring about Lewis's collapse? A good case can be made for this conclusion. How does one explain Lewis's alienation from Thomas Jefferson? His failure to respond to several postexpedition letters to him from his friend Amos Stoddard until just a short time before his death?

William Clark seems to be an exception here. Kushner thinks perhaps their friendship persevered not only because they were both in St. Louis and came into regular contact but because Lewis's risk-taking traits were dominant during the expedition when a true bond with Clark was formed. What of Lewis's risk-taking personality? Lewis was definitely a risk taker. Incidents from early in his career and while on the expedition testify to this. "Placing one's life in constant danger," wrote Kushner, "is . . . a common trait of suicidal personalities." Lewis's risk taking was a "ritualistic attempt to purge those self-destructive urges that appeared time and time again in his life." That is why he seemed so cool when in dire straits.[88] But the purging didn't always succeed. Lewis's habit of extreme risk taking eventually proved unsuccessful in keeping the demons of self-destruction at bay.

The difficulties of his postexpedition career also confirmed his unconscious belief in his own inadequacies, and when the world seemed to judge him as he judged himself, Lewis took his own life. Another view is that the depressed person adopts a "they will miss me when I'm gone" philosophy. By killing themselves they will live on by being missed and remembered by those who rejected them. These people will also then suffer guilt, just as the deceased did, regarding a loved one. In Lewis's case various government officials, various individuals, perhaps a woman, and even his nation were likely the intended targets of his suicide. His comments before dying—he would kill himself before his enemies could and deprive them of the pleasure—are consistent with this theory.

Did Lewis's risk-taking and self-punishment tendencies form a fatal combination? His excessive drinking is viewed as self-inflicted punishment, and suicide is the most extreme form of self-punishment. Many who knew him, including Jefferson, believed Lewis was an alcoholic. When the government rejected some of his bills in the summer of 1809 and everything seemed to unravel, Lewis felt he was being punished, for whatever reason. So, rather than let his enemies and an ungrateful government have the pleasure of destroying him, Lewis decided to do it himself.

Another factor was Lewis's likely unease at a reunion with Jefferson and others whom he had displeased. Would they reject him? What about his mother? He had planned on settling her with him in St. Louis, but those plans were uncertain due to his financial difficulties. Would she reject him? That would be the cruelest rejection of all. Thus, by the late summer and early fall of 1809, Lewis had either exhausted his alternatives for dealing with his problems or they were not available to him. He was going east to face possible if not likely rejections he could not bear. In his tortured mind, only one choice—suicide—was left to him, and he took it.[89]

In 1999 Dr. Kay Jamison included Meriwether Lewis in her book *Night Falls Fast: Understanding Suicide.* A professor of psychiatry at Johns Hopkins University, Jamison is an acknowledged authority on manic-depressive disorder. She suffers from the illness herself and has experienced suicidal episodes. She clearly knows whereof she speaks. Using her years of study, clinical research, her own personal experience, and research on Lewis, Jamison believed he was manic-depressive, and while he was in a state of depression he committed suicide. She believes some people refuse to accept the verdict of suicide because "suicide is at odds with a country's notion of what a hero should be . . . the possibility that Lewis might have killed himself proved unthinkable to many who had never even met him. Derangement . . . seemed, for some, inconsistent with courage, honor, and accomplishment of the first rank." Consequently, "conspiracy theories and speculation about murder cropped up to 'protect' the blackened reputation of the explorer." The creators of those theories and rumors perceived suicide as a dishonorable act instead of just a dreadfully tragic one.[90]

Jamison balanced the opinions of Jefferson, Clark, and others who believed Lewis killed himself with Lewis biographers and writers such as Olin Wheeler, Richard Dillon, and others who argued for homicide. She described Jefferson's biographical profile of Lewis as a "thoughtful and compassionate portrayal of the death of a courageous man." She acknowledged that others disagree. "Some cannot reconcile the outward realities of Lewis's life with his desire to leave it," Jamison observed.[91] She listed the usual sentiments and arguments against suicide, such as it is a disgrace to die by suicide; Lewis was too young or too successful to kill himself; committing suicide is an intrinsically cowardly act and therefore a great and courageous man like Lewis could not have done such a thing; Jefferson would not have appointed Lewis to lead the expedition if he had known of any mental instability in Lewis or his family line; and so on. But it is very likely Jefferson *did* know Lewis's problems and shortcomings and told the truth about his protégé. His knowledge allowed him to gauge Lewis's emotional ups and downs and how they could be controlled. Jefferson's observations were "perceptive, telling, and completely consistent with what is known about restless, energetic, and impetuous temperaments that have an obverse inclination to despair."

All the evidence of Lewis's final months points to suicide, Jamison wrote, so why the convoluted theories of conspiracy, cerebral malaria, and advanced syphilis? In her opinion, none of them hold up to scrutiny but instead reflect the unwillingness to believe that someone as great and courageous as Meriwether Lewis would commit suicide. "But such men do," Jamison concluded. "And the same bold, restless temperament that Jefferson saw in the young Meriwether Lewis can lie uneasily just this side of a restless, deadly despair."[92] Lewis "lived a life of remarkable courage, accomplishment, and vision," Jamison wrote in a letter to the *Washington Post* in 1996 regarding the exhumation of Lewis's remains and the "blot" of suicide. "Suicide is not a blot on anyone's name; it is a tragedy. . . . [I]n the end, for all of us, it is his life that remains."[93]

Well known for his first-person portrayal of Thomas Jefferson and Meriwether Lewis, Clay Jenkinson is also a humanities scholar who has contributed thoughtful and important works to Lewis and Clark historiography. In the course of developing his Jefferson and Lewis personae and in conducting other research, Jenkinson has spent untold hours contemplating the explorer's death. He, like others who contend the explorer took his own life, admits that it is not a certainty that he did but believes that he must have.

Jenkinson's reflections resulted in an in-depth study of Meriwether Lewis's life after his return from the expedition. In this study, entitled *The Character of Meriwether Lewis: "Completely Metamorphosed" in the American West,* Jenkinson concluded, "Meriwether Lewis never fully re-entered American life after his Voyage of Discovery."[94] Like many returning military veterans, astronauts, and others who have experienced major psychological events, Lewis could never quite fit in after his triumphant return from the Pacific. His good friend and co-leader, William Clark, did but not his partner in discovery. Lewis's personality, the expectations he had for himself and others had for him, and events all seemed to combine to cause a downward spiral.

Jenkinson separated his study of Lewis into chapters focusing on certain episodes and character traits, building to the final chapter entitled "Suicide." In it, Jenkinson listed all the problems Lewis faced in the final weeks of his life—the political, financial, and romantic failures and disappointments, the alcohol and drug use, and his failure to write the expedition history. Jenkinson believes Lewis had an enormous superego and engaged in severe self-scrutiny. Add drink, drugs, and depression to such an ego, and it is a formula for tragedy. As Jefferson observed, drink alone would cause "painful reflections . . . in a mind like his."[95] But of Lewis's many problems, which might have been the one that pushed him over the edge to suicide? Jenkinson thinks it was his failure to write the book. In the end, Lewis believed himself unequal to the task. He was afraid of disappointing the public, his mentor Thomas Jefferson, and especially himself. He was simply overwhelmed. "The West was mightier than the pen—at least his pen," Jenkinson wrote. "He could not write prose equal to his own expectations."[96] Lewis's answer? Procrastinate and drink.

Jenkinson believes that when Lewis returned from the expedition, his psychological immune system was weakened and he was emotionally exhausted. (Today he might be diagnosed as suffering from posttraumatic stress disorder.) Consequently, when the crisis of 1808–1809 came, he had no reserves to support or sustain him. Would a wife have helped? Perhaps. Would being closer to Jefferson have helped? Perhaps. Could Clark have saved him? Perhaps, but Clark did what he could while moving ahead with his own life. Thus, Lewis spiraled downward. "His post-expedition course of self-destruction could scarcely have been more rapid or deliberate," Jenkinson observed. "Drugs, alcohol, broken relationships, disturbed friendships, quarrels public and private, and terminal writers' block carried Meriwether Lewis to his death in a miserable hut in Tennessee." Lewis's self-scrutiny and ego played a crucial role in his suicide. In the end, Jenkinson concluded, the explorer looked in "one too many mirrors," and it was his undoing.[97]

We have no suicide note from Lewis, but if he had written one it might have read something like the one left by another man who also chose to end his life in a Tennessee inn three decades later. The man was Peter W. Grayson. Born in 1788 in Kentucky, Grayson seemed to have all that life could offer. He was a lawyer, politician, soldier, and poet. Like Lewis, Grayson also went west. In 1831 he ventured to Texas, where he became a prominent planter and politician who moved in the highest circles. He was a friend of Stephen Austin's and Sam Houston's. He was a leader in the Texas revolution and attorney general of the Texas Republic. In 1838 he was a candidate for the presidency of Texas. The campaign turned into a nasty political fight that proved to be Grayson's undoing. There was also a report of a romantic rejection. Grayson had battled melancholia his whole life; he described it as "a profound secret" he could never divulge. Like Lewis's, his psyche could stand only so much, and this difficult period was too much for him mentally.

In June of 1838, while still a candidate for president, Grayson left Texas for Washington in his capacity as minister plenipotentiary to the United States. On the night of 8 July he stopped at an inn in Bean Station, Tennessee. It was there, as with Lewis at Grinder's Stand, that his demons overcame him. As with Lewis's death, Grayson's was widely reported. Unlike Lewis, Grayson left notes of apology and explanation. The details of his suicide are hauntingly similar to those in the accounts of Lewis's death.[98]

The inn's proprietor reported that when Grayson arrived, he seemed restless and impatient. He asked for a room several times. At dinner he ate nothing but asked for some tea. Later that evening he talked with the innkeeper and appeared composed, although he did complain of a pain over his eyes. He went to bed at the usual hour and in the morning had a servant at the inn clean his boots. A half-full vial of laudanum was on a table, and the boy later reported that Grayson seemed very sleepy. Eight or ten minutes after the boy left the room, a pistol shot was heard. At first it was thought to have sounded from outside, but when Grayson didn't come down for breakfast, a servant girl took food up to him, whereupon she found him dead on the floor. He had put a pistol to his head and blown his brains out. Among his effects was his will, a note of apology to the innkeeper for the "frightful scene I have made in your house," a letter of farewell to his friends, and a statement of explanation. If Lewis had left a note, perhaps it might have read something like Grayson's:

> *To my friends.* I go to my grave for the quiet the world can never give me. The fiend that pursued me for a long time previous to 1830, and then let me rest, ('twas when I went to Texas,) has started on me again with redoubled fury. To save myself from the horrors of the madhouse, I go to my grave. Farewell! To you and the few kindred of my particular affections I yield the last pulsations of my heart.[99]

Grayson then wrote another note, a page and a half in length, explaining his desperate situation and drastic action. "It is necessary to my poor shattered name for me now to confess that at least ten years of my life I have been a partially deranged man," he wrote. "I have always kept this a profound secret, from an indescribable horror I have ever felt at the idea of divulging it." Through the period of his worst suffering, 1820 to 1830, his mood was "disqualifying and adverse to mental exertion of any kind." Still he worked on a publishing project in "hope of bringing my mind back to something like sanity again by a strong desperate effort at mental energy." His move to Texas had enabled him to rally, but then the old demons returned. "This I write in my last hours of existence. I sincerely think as a sane or living man. Whether I shall be in Bedlam or my grave soon, I know not: I am in the hands of malignant fate, and the worst that can befall me will, I am sure." After signing the note P. W. G., he added, "the last trap to catch my soul, and send it to a very hell of torture, was the good feeling of my friends, urging me and prevailing on me to be a candidate for the presidency of Texas! Oh, God!!"[100]

The parallels to Meriwether Lewis are startling. Change a few words and one can almost imagine the famous explorer writing a very similar farewell to his friends in his room at Grinder's Stand, signing his last words with the initials M. L.

Was Meriwether Lewis murdered or did he kill himself? Did the "waight of his mind" overcome him in that backwoods Tennessee inn? The evidence strongly supports suicide. It was the verdict in 1809 and it should still be the verdict two hundred years later.

# Notes

1. Coues, *History*, 1:lxi.

2. Alexander Wilson, "Particulars," 39.

3. Jenkinson, *Character of Meriwether Lewis*, 111–14.

4. Jackson, *Letters*, 2:415, 681–84; Ambrose, *Undaunted Courage*, 421–28.

5. Jackson, *Letters*, 2:415, 418.

6. Ibid., 720, 721n; Ambrose, *Undaunted Courage*, 427–31; Jenkinson, *Character of Meriwether Lewis*, 33–40.

7. Marshall, *Life and Papers*, 2:64.

8. Ibid., 67–68.

9. Ibid., 69.

10. Ibid., 75, 100–101.

11. Ibid., 109–12.

12. Jackson, *Letters*, 2:459–61.

13. Ibid., 459–62, 728–31; Holmberg, *Dear Brother*, 209–10. Both Grace Lewis Miller and Ruth Colter-Frick argue unconvincingly that Lewis was *not* in financial difficulty but was solvent. It should also be noted that both women were supporters of the murder theory and used sources selectively. See Miller, letter of 16 December 1956, Grace Lewis Miller Papers; Colter-Frick, "Meriwether Lewis's Personal Finances," 16–20.

14. Jackson, *Letters*, 2:464–67. It is debated whether Lewis's 16 September 1809 letter to Madison was indeed posted to the president or is an unsent draft. Jackson listed it as being the recipient's copy (thus actually sent to Madison), but murder theorists claim it is only a draft. The letter lacks an address leaf, thereby depriving researchers of an important clue—if not definitive evidence—as to whether it was sent. But there are two bits of evidence that convincingly indicate it was sent. The letter is docketed, or endorsed, a method commonly used at that time by recipients to indicate the writer of the letter and when it was written or received. And, most importantly, according to David Mattern, senior associate editor of the *Papers of James Madison*, the handwriting of the docket, while not Madison's, matches that of many other endorsements on letters in the Madison Papers at the Library of Congress. This letter of Lewis's is cited in the first volume of the presidential series of the *Papers of James Madison* as being the recipient's copy. Therefore, Lewis's 16 September letter was clearly received by Madison, and it must be assumed that it was intentionally sent by Lewis. David Mattern in personal communication, 3 October 2005.

15. Holmberg, *Dear Brother*, 230n; Russell Family data, Townsend Genealogical Database; Pilcher, *Historical Sketches*, 17, 35. Russell County, Alabama, was named for Gilbert Russell upon its formation on 18 December 1832. Russell had actually been promoted to the rank of major in May 1809. It probably was retroactive because he was referred to as a captain in the fall of 1809. (See Heitman, *Historical Register*, 1:853.)

16. Holmberg, *Dear Brother*, 228.

17. Russell to Jefferson, 4 January 1810, Thomas Jefferson Papers, Library of Congress, online collection, images 487–90. Also see Jackson, *Letters*, 2:574–75n.

18. Russell to Jefferson, 31 January 1810, Thomas Jefferson Papers, online collection, images 568–70. Also see Jackson, *Letters*, 2:575n. Donald Jackson, an eminent Lewis and Clark scholar, deemed the words of this letter "depressingly persuasive" evidence of suicide.

19. Russell to Jefferson, 31 January 1810.

20. Statement of Gilbert Russell, 26 November 1811, Jonathan Williams Manuscripts, Lilly Library, Indiana University. Also see Jackson, *Letters*, 2:573–74, for a transcript of the statement. Jonathan Williams, who was a jurist as well as a soldier, had connections with Lewis not only through membership in the American Philosophical Society but through association with Thomas Jefferson himself. See Heitman, *Historical Register*, 1:1041, regarding Williams.

21. Russell statement, 26 November 1811.

22. Ibid.

23. Jackson, *Letters*, 2:467–68; Neelly to Jefferson, 18 October 1809, Thomas Jefferson Papers, online collection, images 318–21.

24. Holmberg, *Dear Brother*, 225n.

25. Jackson, "On the Death," 445–48.

26. Holmberg, *Dear Brother*, 228, 231n.

27. John Brahan to Thomas Jefferson, 18 October 1809, Thomas Jefferson Papers, online collection, images 312–15.

28. Jackson, "On the Death," 445–48. On 5 May 1810 Sueverman wrote Thomas Jefferson of Pernier's death and the circumstances surrounding it.

29. Brahan to Jefferson, 18 October 1809.

30. Ibid. Brahan also wrote Amos Stoddard on 18 October 1809, informing him that Lewis had killed himself and relating most of the same information, but not as much detail, as he related to Jefferson. See Thwaites, *Original Journals*, 7:389.

31. Holmberg, *Dear Brother*, 209–10, 212–13.

32. Ibid., 210, 212–14.

33. Ibid., 216–18. Clark's 28 October 1809 letter was not written at expedition veteran George Shannon's house as is sometimes stated. See 219–20.

34. Guice, "Fatal Rendezvous," 11; Chuinard, "How Did Meriwether Lewis Die?" 18:2, 7.

35. Holmberg, *Dear Brother*, 224.

36. Ibid., 225–26.

37. Ibid., 228.

38. Jackson, *Letters*, 2:591–92. Jefferson's biographical profile of Lewis, written in 1813 and published in 1814 as the foreword to Biddle and Allen's *History*, can also be viewed online in the Thomas Jefferson Papers.

39. Jackson, *Letters*, 2:592.

40. Ibid., 592–93.

41. Ibid., 474–75.

42. Jefferson to William D. Meriwether, 21 August 1810, Thomas Jefferson Papers, online collection, image 1082.

43. Jackson, *Letters*, 2:728.

44. Ibid., 469.

45. Ibid., 487–91; Jefferson to Meriwether, 21 August 1810; Holmberg, *Dear Brother*, 232.

46. Marshall, *Life and Papers*, 2:101, 108–12. Also see Ambrose, *Undaunted Courage*, 459.

47. *St. Louis Missouri Gazette*, 23 November 1809.

48. *Nashville (Tenn.) Democratic Clarion*, 20 October 1809.

49. *Russellville (Ky.) Farmer's Friend*, 27 October 1809. The account might have come from the *Impartial Review and Cumberland Repository*, published 1805–1809. There was also a paper named the *Nashville (Tenn.) Intelligencer*, which began publishing in 1799 and ended at an undetermined date.

50. *St. Louis Missouri Gazette*, 2 November 1809.

51. Thwaites, *Original Journals*, 7:391.

52. Alexander Wilson, "Particulars,"37–40. A portion of Wilson's letter and poem can also be read in Dillon, *Meriwether Lewis* (1965), 339–41, and "Alexander Wilson's Report on Lewis's Death" in *We Proceeded On*, 28:24. It is interesting to note the significant liberties that Dillon takes in regard to Wilson's account.

53. Coues, *History*, 1:lxi.

54. Jackson, *Among Sleeping Giants*, 35–36.

55. Kennerly and Russell, *Persimmon Hill*, 27.

56. Sally Lewis Anderson to Eva Emery Dye, 16 April 1902, Eva Emery Dye Papers; Mary Starling Payne to Lyman C. Draper, 18 March 1890, 34CC50, Draper Manuscripts; E. C. Lewis, "Meriwether Lewis' Death"; McCallister and Tandy, *Genealogies*, 46–47; William Lewis, *Genealogy*, 52–53; Wheeler, *Trail*, 1: 6–68; Bakeless, *Lewis and Clark*, 425; *Philadelphia Saturday American*, 7 December 1844.

57. *Philadelphia Saturday American*, 7 December 1844; *New York Dispatch*, 1 February 1845. The *Dispatch* most likely picked the story up from the *Saturday American*; the two stories are very similar. The *Saturday American* reportedly got the story from the *Batesville North Arkansas*.

58. Russell statement, 26 November 1811. Also see Jackson, *Letters*, 2:573.

59. Coues, *History*, 1:xliii–lxii; Park, "Meriwether Lewis." Park used the pseudonym John Quill. The article was originally published in the *Nashville American* on 6 September 1891. The historical importance of the article was considered such that with the approach of the 1904 Louisiana Purchase Exposition it was reprinted in the 4 January 1903 edition of the *American*. (I have used the 1903 reprint because a copy of the 1891 article could not be

located.) Coues's commentary/notes in his expedition history contain a very Anglocentric view of society. He belittled, among others, Indians, French people, and Paul Allen, the editor of what is known as the "Biddle edition" of the expedition journals, published in 1814. For specific examples regarding this, see Chalkley, "Paul Allen," 8–11.

60. Park, "Meriwether Lewis." Also see Coues, *History*, 1:liii–liv.

61. Park, "Meriwether Lewis." Also see Coues, *History*, 1:lv.

62. Jackson, *Letters*, 2:470–72.

63. Alexander Wilson, "Particulars,"38.

64. Coues, *History*, 1:lvi.

65. Ibid., xlvii–xlviii.

66. Webster, "Death of Gen. Lewis." The identity of the Robert O. Smith who claimed to be the post rider that morning has long been questioned. Census records cite a Robert O. Smith of Maury County, Tennessee, as being forty-three years old in 1850—born therefore about 1806. There is another Robert Smith living in Maury County who was sixty-nine in 1850 and was thus born about 1780. By the time Webster could have interviewed the elder Smith, he would have been at least eighty and probably older. The younger Smith would have been around sixty or older and is thought to be Webster's source. Perhaps something got jumbled in the retelling as to who the post rider actually was (if indeed there was one). Or perhaps the younger Smith spun quite a convincing yarn that Webster swallowed.

67. Wheeler, *Trail*; Bakeless, *Lewis and Clark*; Fisher, *Suicide or Murder?*; Dillon, *Meriwether Lewis* (1965); Chuinard, "How Did Meriwether Lewis Die?"; Chandler, *Jefferson Conspiracies*.

68. Dillon, *Meriwether Lewis* (1965), 344, 350.

69. Jackson, *Letters*, 2:748; Jackson, *Among Sleeping Giants*, 69–70.

70. *Coroner's Inquest*, Starrs testimony, 11–42.

71. *Coroner's Inquest*, Guice testimony, 63–100; Bakeless, *Lewis and Clark*, 423; Dillon, *Meriwether Lewis* (1965), 333. Also see Guice, "Fatal Rendezvous," 4–12. For more on Guice's support of Vardis Fisher and his murder contention, see Guice, "Fisher and Meriwether Lewis."

72. Guice, "Moonlight and Meriwether Lewis," 21–23.

73. John Moore, "Death of Meriwether Lewis," 218–30.

74. Ibid., 224.

75. Ibid., 224–25.

76. Ibid., 225.

77. Ibid., 225–26.

78. Ibid., 227; Jackson, *Letters*, 2:467–68.

79. Ibid., 228–29.

80. Ibid., 230.

81. Phelps, "Tragic Death," 305–318; the quoted passage appears on pages 317–18.

82. Jackson, *Letters*, 2:575n.

83. Cutright, "Rest, Rest, Perturbed Spirit," 7–16.

84. Ravenholt, "Triumph Then Despair," 366–79. Ravenholt used this piece as the basis of other articles.

85. Danisi, "Ague," 10–15.

86. Peck, *Or Perish*, 292.

87. Kushner, "Suicide," 464–81.

88. Ibid., 479.

89. Ibid., 479–81.

90. Jamison, *Night Falls Fast*, 220.

91. Ibid., 225–26.

92. Ibid., 229.

93. Ibid., 230.

94. Jenkinson, *Character of Meriwether Lewis*, 1.

95. Ibid., 103.

96. Ibid., 104–105.

97. Ibid., 115–16.

98. *Niles' National Register*, 54:394; Southwick, "Peter Wagener Grayson." In yet another eerie connection, *Niles'* published the account on 18 August 1838, what would have been Meriwether Lewis's sixty-fourth birthday.

99. *Niles' National Register*, 54:394.

100. Ibid., 394–95.

# CHAPTER TWO

# "It Seems to Be More Probable . . .":

*Why Not Homicide?*

## JOHN D. W. GUICE

Because historians inevitably bring to their work the biases of their academic and personal experiences, it is important to reveal here the origins of my interest in this inquiry. When I began work in the 1980s with Thomas D. Clark on a book about the Old Southwest, I had forgotten that Meriwether Lewis died on the Natchez Trace.[1] However, as we wrote the chapter on the trace, we of course addressed the time, place, and violent nature of his demise. Indeed, only then did I recall the vague memory of hearing my father, more than three decades earlier, refer to the "suicide" of Meriwether Lewis. My point is that I began my inquiry with as clean a slate as one could imagine—free from any ideas inculcated by mentors or colleagues.

After our book on the Old Southwest was in press, I began research for a history of the Natchez Trace, and as I delved into the literature, I found it curious that so many historians declared unequivocally that Lewis had killed himself. Their acceptance of suicide on such flimsy circumstantial evidence—all based ultimately on hearsay—motivated my rather prolonged investigation into as many aspects of this historio-graphical challenge as seemed reasonable. I had a lot to learn abut the Lewis and Clark Expedition, but on the other hand, I knew a lot more about the Natchez Trace than most persons writing about the death of Lewis. No one knows whether or not Meriwether Lewis committed suicide. No one witnessed the firing of the two .69 calibre pistol balls that caused the fatal wounds. There are plenty of arguments to counter the claims offered by the proponents of suicide. Hence the theme of this essay: Why not homicide?

Any discussion of Governor Lewis's final hours begins with the ac-counts related by Priscilla Grinder to Major James Neely and Alex-ander Wilson, although other versions of her memories of the occasion appeared much later. Neely wrote to Thomas Jefferson from Nashville on 18 October, a week after the event, that Lewis had died "by suicide." Wilson, the noted ornithologist, visited the grave of his friend in late winter or early spring of 1811. His letter of 28 May 1811 from Natchez, based on notes from his interview with Mrs. Grinder, provides the most often quoted account of what happened the night of 10–11 October 1809. (See Document 8 in the Documents section of this book.)

The essential elements of Wilson's letter are these: Lewis arrived at the stand ahead of the two servants; he asked for some "spirits" but drank very little; he asked the servant for his gunpowder; he paced back and forth, at times "speaking to himself in a violent manner"; he ate "only a few mouthfuls," smoked his pipe, and commented, "Madam this is a very pleasant evening"; he expressed a desire to sleep on his buffalo robe; the servants retired to a barn two hundred yards off; Mrs. Grinder went to another log cabin, the kitchen, a few paces away; from there she could hear Lewis pacing back and forth in the guest cabin for several hours, talking "like a lawyer."

Wilson's letter continues: Then Mrs. Grinder heard a pistol shot, heard something fall to floor, heard the words "O Lord!" and then a second shot. She heard Lewis call out, "O madam! give me some water, and heal my wounds." She peered through the cracks between the logs and saw him staggering around between the two cabins; he returned to his cabin and then came to her door. She heard him scraping an empty bucket in a plea for water, but gave him none; terrified, she rendered no aid for two hours. Finally, she sent her two children to rouse the ser-vants, who found him on his bed. Lewis showed the servants a bullet wound on his side; in addition, they observed that a piece of his forehead was blown off, exposing his brain. Lewis begged them to shoot him with his rifle, repeating the words, "I am no coward, but I am *so* strong, *so hard to die.*" He died "just as the sun rose above the trees."

Unlike Wilson's letter, Neely's letter to Jefferson related the details of his journey with Lewis from Fort Pickering to Grinder's Stand, Lewis's burial, and the disposal of the governor's possessions. (See Document 4.) However, the three sentences quoted most often from Neely's letter are

1. "And on our arrival at the Chickasaw nation I discovered that he appeared at times deranged in mind."
2. ". . . and no person there but a woman who discovering the governor to be deranged gave him up the house & slept herself in one near it."
3. ". . . when his servant came in he says; I have done the business my good servant give me some water."

Even though Neely's message was based on hearsay, not an eyewitness account, many historians accept his letter at face value. Note that, according to Wilson's report, Mrs. Grinder made no reference either to an assassin or to the victim's killing himself. Neely is the first person of record to use the term "suicide." It is also important to note that neither Wilson nor Neely mentioned razor cuts to Lewis's body. Though a rumor of razor cuts mysteriously surfaced only later, some writers refer to the cuts as established "fact."

Collectively, proponents of suicide offer a multitude of arguments, most of which are designed to show in one way or another that depression drove Lewis to take his own life. They view his delay in reporting to St. Louis as an indication that Lewis was despondent over his failure to find a wife. Consequently, he became an alcoholic. Then, his inability as governor to cope with administrative affairs—combined with his financial difficulties in St. Louis—led to further despondence and/or depression. Curiously, even his writing of a will at New Madrid is interpreted as evidence of impending suicide.

Those who subscribe to the suicide theory also interpret events that transpired at Fort Pickering as indicators that Governor Lewis was not in his right mind when he arrived there. According to Captain Russell, commanding officer at Fort Pickering, the boat crew reported that Lewis had tried twice to kill himself. Russell initially wrote that Lewis had arrived at the fort in a state of "indisposition" due to overconsumption of alcohol. Then two years later, Russell described his condition as one of "mental derangement." The corrections and uncertain hand in a letter that Lewis wrote from Fort Pickering to President Madison may also indicate emotional instability. (See Document 2.)

Those historians who persist in the belief the Lewis pulled the trigger also base their position on the fact that Thomas Jefferson accepted the initial report of suicide and that in 1814 he wrote that "Governor Lewis had been from early lifetime subject to hypochondriac affections" which Jefferson attributed to "a constitutional disposition in all branches of the family."[2] Others who share that view place great stock in the insistence of some historians that William Clark, co-captain on the expedition, allegedly accepted the report of suicide.[3]

A variety of other arguments are offered. For instance, Howard Kushner in his 1981 psychoanalytic inquiry attributes the assumed suicide to childhood mental trauma, although he admits that up to 1981 most scholars believe someone murdered Lewis.[4] Then there is the contention by park historian Dawson Phelps that the Natchez Trace "was not, in 1809, a dangerous place."[5] Another recurring theme is that Lewis made no progress on the editing of his journals while in St. Louis and seldom wrote Jefferson while he was there, indicators that Lewis suffered from depression. One of the more recent entries into the suicide-homicide fray is the theory that Lewis killed himself while suffering from the agonizing tertiary effects of syphilis.[6]

These arguments for suicide are readily countered. I address first the conviction that Lewis's delay in reporting to St. Louis indicates that he was depressed. Actually, Lewis conducted a considerable amount of important business in Philadelphia related to the publication of the journals as well as to a volume of scientific data collected during the expedition to the Pacific.[7] For instance, he met with two botanists, Dr. Benjamin Smith Barton and his German-born protégé Frederick Pursh. He contracted with Alexander Wilson to draw birds, Charles Willson Peale to paint portraits of other animals, and Irish-born engraver John James Barralet to illustrate the Great Falls of the Missouri and the Falls of the Columbia. There were also negotiations with French artist Charles B. J. F. De St. Memin, whom he paid to do likenesses of Indians. (Though their drawings and portraits did not appear in the first edition of the Lewis and Clark journals published in 1814, they survived and subsequently graced the pages of numerous other publications.)

Because Lewis was not adequately trained in the use of navigational instruments, some of his measurements of latitude and longitude required corrections, and for this task he engaged a mathematician from the U.S. Military Academy at West Point, Ferdinand Rudolph Hassler. One can safely assume that in Philadelphia Lewis also visited Woodland, the estate of well-known gardener William Hamilton. Jefferson had sent Hamilton some of the seeds shipped by Lewis and Clark from Fort Mandan.

In preparation for the expedition in 1803, Lewis had conferred with numerous experts in Philadelphia such as the famous medical doctor Benjamin Rush, anatomy professor Caspar Wistar, and mathematician Robert Patterson, who gave him a quick course on the use of the quadrant, sextant, and chronometer. There were others as well. How could he have resisted conversations with them in 1807 in order to express his gratitude and to discuss problems he encountered in the West? Indeed, these men undoubtedly looked forward to entertaining their most famous pupil. And who knows how many members of the American Philosophical Society extended invitations to Lewis when he attended its meetings in April, June, and July?

Virtually every commentary on the newly appointed governor's Philadelphia interlude mentions the renewal of his friendship with Mahlon Dickerson. Invariably these accounts emphasize Lewis's letter back to Dickerson from Virginia complaining about the futility of his quest there for a spouse. On the other hand, however, why not point to the many good times Lewis and Dickerson most likely shared as they cavorted with the girls and exchanged stories with other bachelors in one of America's most interesting cities? One does not have to be a veteran of the armed forces to easily imagine how welcome such an opportunity would have been to a healthy young man after so many months in the West without feminine companionship.

Only a person *searching* for depression could measure these weeks in Philadelphia in terms of depression. One of the symptoms of depression is inactivity. Clearly, Lewis during this interlude was on the move. Paul Russell Cutright, who was a leading authority on Lewis's activities in Philadelphia, asks, "Why did Lewis needlessly prolong his stay in Philadelphia?" Cutright sees the answer in frustration and alcoholism. I choose to see fun and frolic as the answer. Later, after he found such huge challenges in St. Louis, Lewis probably regretted the length of this interlude, but while he was there chances are that he thoroughly enjoyed himself.

After departing the City of Brotherly Love, Lewis conferred again with President Thomas Jefferson en route to Virginia. There he attended the trial of Aaron Burr in Richmond as Jefferson's personal observer before revisiting family at their homestead. Yes, he actively, but unsuccessfully, sought a wife in Virginia as well as in Philadelphia. So have countless other men throughout the ages. Historians read entirely too much into the fact that Lewis did not tie the nuptial knot. Lewis's East Coast interlude was a dalliance, not a delay. Most likely, after three years in the wilderness, Lewis was indulging himself.

Standard among the arguments in favor of suicide are charges that Lewis was an alcoholic. Yes, he at times did drink. It is safe to say that at times he got drunk, and one of those times may have been on his arrival at Fort Pickering. But drinking in the young republic, and especially on the frontier, was par at a time when par was pretty high. The amount of whiskey drunk on the southern frontier seems astronomical by modern standards. One of the primary products shipped down the Mississippi in flatboats was whiskey; it was the drink of choice among travelers on the Natchez Trace. In the American army, as in all armies, both enlisted men and officers enjoyed alcoholic beverages of one form or another. Notice how much of it Lewis and Clark took with them; everyone shared it. Where is the *hard* evidence that Meriwether Lewis was an alcoholic? Many writers echo the charge of alcoholism, but none point to creditable evidence. In an 1810 reply to Gilbert Russell, who had written that Lewis was intoxicated on his arrival at Chickasaw Bluffs, Jefferson made a cryptic reference to "the habit into which he [Lewis] had fallen."[8] But that isolated comment hardly constitutes sufficient evidence to declare anything definitive about Lewis.

Taking into account the interference of Frederick Bates, Lewis handled administrative affairs in St. Louis quite well, especially those relating to the Indians. With its French, Spanish, and American heritages, and with its large American Indian population, Upper Louisiana was far more complex than most territories. Richard Dillon, in his superb 1965 biography, summarized the complexities and intrigue that characterized this territory in the opening paragraph of his chapter entitled "His Excellency":

Meriwether Lewis did not realize what he was getting into as Governor of Upper Louisiana. The old Franco-Spanish town of St. Louis which he had known was gone, revolutionized during his absence by the immigration of Americans from across the Mississippi. Daily the little capital became more sophisticated, turning its political face toward Washington rather than westward up the Missouri. Politicians, speculators and out-and-out peculators crowded into the territory to fatten on the new pickings there in land fraud and Indian trade. Violence, deceit and character assassination became the guidelines of sociopolitical activity with, as always, basic economic motives lying at the bottom of every scrape.[9]

Scholars who have spent much time researching and writing the history of trans-Mississippi territories must wonder if President Jefferson fully realized the difficulties facing anyone who attempted to govern such a terribly complex territory. If the president removed Lewis's predecessor, James Wilkinson, because of his ineffectiveness, could he possibly have expected Lewis to quickly produce a manuscript for publication of the journals? It would have been utterly unrealistic on Jefferson's part to anticipate that anyone assigned such a demanding administrative task could or would quickly complete such an editorial assignment. Undoubtedly the delay in publishing the journals disappointed Lewis, but it is not likely that he was despondent as a result. Reference to Lewis's despondence as a result of this delay is just another example of searching for "evidence" to support the suicide hypothesis.

Considering the tremendous expenditure of time and energy spent by Lewis—even with the able assistance of Clark—in contending with innumerable challenges posed by the presence of such a large and varied Indian population in the territory, it is difficult to fathom why some writers give Lewis poor marks for his role as governor. Undoubtedly, Lewis himself regretted that he did not arrive on the scene earlier. One must not believe that he was oblivious to his territorial responsibilities while he remained on the eastern seaboard, for he attempted, with little success, to direct certain territorial affairs in correspondence with Bates. As even his sympathetic biographer Dillon writes, "This was an impossible task, an incredible folly."[10]

Though Bates had performed reasonably well in Lewis's absence, he badly botched Indian affairs. Lewis recognized even from a distance of over seven hundred miles that Bates was inadequately prepared in this area and instructed him by mail to defer decisions regarding Indian policy to Clark, Pierre Chouteau, and to himself. Unfortunately, Bates, who had earlier admitted to Lewis his ineptness in such matters, ignored Lewis's advice. While the governor concentrated his efforts on the resolution of tribal problems, he paid attention to the myriad other administrative tasks before him. Pro-suicide writers who speculate wildly that he fell apart emotionally in St. Louis and that he was incapable of functioning as governor are simply grasping at straws. This is not to say that he was a popular governor. As Dillon points out, he faced an intensely contentious constituency that included powerful figures jockeying for economic advantage, and Bates took full advantage of this fact to undermine Lewis at every opportunity. On this virtually all historians agree. In other words, Bates is not a reliable source through which to judge Lewis's performance in St. Louis.

Next we turn to the popular assertion that another contribution to Lewis's suicide was his despair over his finances, especially should his appeal to the War Department fall on unsympathetic ears. Yes, Lewis had a momentary cash flow problem, but he stood to make a lot of money from his investments in land, and he surely recognized that fact. Territorial officials on both sides of the Mississippi River dealt in the widest range of speculation; they sought those low-paying jobs because of investment opportunities. And like Lewis, throughout the trans-Mississippi West officials constantly battled uninformed, parsimonious bureaucrats in Washington, D.C. Indeed, in this respect, Lewis had plenty of company.

On 28 May 1999 in Sioux Falls, South Dakota, just months before her untimely death, Ruth Colter-Frick read an excellent paper entitled "The Myth of Insolvency: The Financial Affairs of Governor Meriwether Lewis at the Time of His Death." She based her research on the Grace Lewis Miller Collection at the Jefferson National Expansion Memorial Archives in St. Louis, Missouri, as well as on documents from eight other repositories spread across the nation. Colter-Frick proved that, while Lewis clearly had a temporary cash flow problem, he was far from bankrupt. He had invested carefully in valuable land holdings in St. Louis with an eye toward moving his mother there, and in addition, the governor owned significant assets in other parts of the country.[11] Yes, he faced temporary financial embarrassment, and some of his St. Louis creditors hastened to call in their loans on the news of the pressures he faced because of the War Department's denial of some of his claims. But, contrary to what is often written, Lewis was definitely not bankrupt.

As the son of an attorney and the brother of several other attorneys, I find it strange that scholars interpret the writing of a will at New Madrid as an indication of contemplated suicide. From childhood I was taught that every adult should prepare a will. While all of us procrastinate, only a terribly imprudent man, facing a sea voyage at any time, but especially just before the War of 1812, would *not* write a will. On its face, this "evidence" of suicide is specious. Governor Lewis knew he had considerable assets that he wished to bequeath to his mother.

Next I address briefly the 26 November 1811 statement of Captain Russell. In this report Russell related that he learned from the boat crew "that he [Lewis] had made two attempts to Kill himself, in one of which he had nearly succeeded." Considering the rather detailed nature of his statement, it is curious that Captain Russell offered no details of the alleged suicide attempts en route to Memphis. Had Lewis inflicted wounds upon his own body, it seems that Russell would have commented to that effect. In addition to being the chief executive of a gigantic territory, Governor Lewis was truly a national hero. Hence, it is odd that the boatmen did not give the particulars to the commanding officer of Fort Pickering. In the absence of references by Russell to any physical injuries, it is fair to assume that the crew told Russell that Lewis had jumped overboard. Or did he lose his balance and fall from the deck as it rocked back and forth due to wind and current on one of the world's greatest rivers?

On 16 September 1809, just one day after arriving at the fort, Meriwether Lewis wrote a brief letter to President James Madison. He explained why he had changed his mind about a sea voyage, that instead he was traveling by land via Tennessee, that he felt confident the administration would accept his explanations, and that he was anxious to resume his duties as governor. With his letter Lewis transmitted a copy of recently printed territorial laws. The governor justifiably was quite proud of this publication, which he considered a major achievement of his administration. Because the extant copy of the letter contains numerous corrections, suicide proponents argue that it indicates that at Fort Pickering Lewis was mentally unstable. A person not seeking to support a hypothesis of self-destruction, however, could easily take the letter at face value. Not only does the text clearly indicate that he was rational, but parts of it are upbeat and optimistic for one who arrived just a day earlier a rather sick man.[12]

Furthermore, among other pieces of business he tended to at Fort

Pickering, Lewis wrote his former army comrade Amos Stoddard, who was then stationed at Fort Adams, just south of Natchez, to let Stoddard know of his change of plans. He expressed confidence that he would prevail in Washington. "An explanation is all that is necessary I am sensible to put all matters right."[13] Then Lewis asked Stoddard to send to Washington two hundred dollars that he was holding for him so the money would arrive while he was there. (See Document 3.) This does not sound like a man contemplating suicide!

At this point it is important to refer to the 1996 coroner's inquest in Hohenwald, Tennessee, county seat of Lewis County, where Lewis is buried. His grave lies beneath a monument on the site of Grinder's Stand, now part of the Natchez Trace Parkway administered by the National Park Service. For most of two days, fourteen witnesses testified under oath before a large crowd in a National Guard armory. In addition to two historians, the witnesses included experts in the fields of geology, document examination, forensic psychology, forensic pathology, forensic anthropology, firearms, and wound ballistics. The transcript contains 364 pages. One can summarize their testimony as follows: It is likely that sufficient skeletal remains exist to permit a forensic examination; such an examination is practical without disturbing the monument; and it could rule out suicide.

Document experts at the inquest testified that the extant copy of Lewis's letter to Madison from Fort Pickering is merely a rough draft, bearing no signs of mental deterioration. A highly qualified certified forensic document examiner studied nine samples of known writings by Meriwether Lewis, five by Gilbert Russell, and one by Jonathan Williams in whose papers one of Russell's most often cited documents was found. Russell's 1811 statement contains an inscription at the end under his own signature that reads: "The above was received by me from Major Gilbert Russell of the [blank] Regiment of Infantry U.S. on Tuesday the 26th of November 1811 at Fredericktown in Maryland. Signed J. Williams."

The attorney who questioned document expert Gerald B. Richards focused on the letter that Lewis wrote to President Madison from Fort Pickering:

Q: Now, do you find anything unusual about the writing in this 1809 letter compared to the 1807 document and the other 1809 letter to his friend Amos [Stoddard]?

A: As far as the writing goes, the style of writing, the relative size, the speed, the quality of what we call the rhythm of the writing, it's all totally consistent with the other two examples. The only difference[,] and it's a very noticeable difference, is there are numerous—and this is what the historians mostly dwelled on—there are numerous corrections, cross outs, additions, deletions throughout the entire document; however, the handwriting itself is stable, it is as solid as he has ever written it before.[14]

Another fascinating part of the testimony dealt with Gilbert Russell's statement of 26 November 1811—the one in which Russell described Lewis as mentally deranged on arrival at the fort and in which he mentioned the alleged suicide attempts by Lewis on the boat. This statement was found in the papers of Jonathan Williams, who purportedly wrote on the bottom of the document that Russell sent it to him, that is, Williams.[15] This statement is another cornerstone of the argument for suicide. The expert testified, however, that "based on these characteristics and numerous other ones I found throughout the writing, it became very obvious that Russell did not write the Russell statement that's purported to describe what happened to Meriwether Lewis. . . . Williams did not write the Russell signature. . . . Neither he [Williams] nor the purported writer of it who signed at the bottom wrote those particular documents."[16]

Perhaps Russell dictated the statement. While it was not unusual for secretaries or other associates to transcribe letters, unless otherwise indicated by the transcriber, the author would have signed it. The second document examiner was Dr. Duayne Dillon, an expert witness in hundreds of cases. Neither expert, Gerald Richards or Duayne Dillon, knew the other was examining the same set of documents—actually photographic copies of documents. Dillon confirmed that the 1811 statement attributed to Gilbert Russell was not written by either Russell or Jonathan Williams. Nor were their signatures authentic. Hence, these conclusions by two highly reputable experts cast great doubt on the authenticity of one of the key documents cited by proponents of the suicide theory—Russell's 26 November 1811 statement.

Dillon also testified regarding the letters written by Lewis at Fort Pickering. According to him, the signatures of Lewis at the fort were "actually superior to many of the other signatures." Likewise, the writing in the text of the letters just before Lewis's death showed no deterioration—"no change at all." Furthermore, Dillon, who has done experimental work on the effect of alcohol consumption on writing, found no such effects in the writing of Lewis at Fort Pickering.[17] Undoubtedly, some of those persons who doggedly subscribe to the suicide theory have read neither the transcript of the 1996 inquest nor publications quoting it. Nevertheless, this testimony causes me to exclaim, "How dare some of our colleagues proclaim that no questions remain regarding the circumstances surrounding the death of Lewis!"

This testimony vindicates Vardis Fisher's opinion of the Russell statement. Donald Jackson provided Fisher a transcription of the Russell statement in 1960, prior to the publication of Fisher's 1962 study. When he read it, Fisher wrote back that it had fallen upon him like a "bombshell," but he doubted its authenticity:

> I read half the first page and was so astonished that I went back and reread, knowing that if this is authentic it overthrows my thesis that Lewis did not kill himself. Somewhere early in the second page I was strongly feeling that Gilbert Russell never wrote this, and by the time I reached the end of it, I was convinced that he did not. It is so unlike what he wrote in two letters to Jefferson in its spirit, in its use of the language, and in its statements of what happened. So the question in my mind is, Who wrote it and why? For if Russell wrote it, he had in two years completely changed his attitude toward Lewis and his view of what happened.[18]

In light of the testimony of two document experts, studying the material independently and without any collaboration whatever, Fisher's perception thirty-six years earlier was remarkably prescient, to say the least. Indeed, his response to Jackson gives us considerable insight into Fisher himself. And the testimony of the document's examiners discredits some of his critics.[19]

My test of the arguments for suicide continues with further examination of the letter that Neelly wrote to Jefferson informing him of Lewis's death. In his description of the fatal journey, Neelly included this observation on the condition of his traveling companion: "And on our arrival at the Chickasaw nation I discovered that he appeared at times deranged." Undoubtedly, Lewis was exhausted after the ride of some one hundred miles in the heat from Fort Pickering to the Chickasaw Agency on the Natchez Trace near the present town of Houston, Mississippi. If he was "at times deranged," it may have been just a symptom of his exhaustion, because at the agency Lewis wrote a totally rational note for delivery by another traveler to Russell. His message contained instructions on the disposition of the excess baggage that Lewis had left at Fort Pickering.[20] Since travelers on the Natchez Trace often fell ill, it is conceivable that, rather than actually being out of his mind, Lewis suffered from heatstroke or a malaria attack. For that matter, both Lewis and Neelly could have been drinking too much.

To many, the most convincing evidence that Lewis was not murdered is that Thomas Jefferson left no written objection to the report of suicide from Neelly. Because no record exists of Jefferson's meeting with Pernier, we do not know his initial reaction. But he did not publicly call for an investigation into Lewis's death. Jefferson's decisions to hire Lewis as his secretary, to select him as leader of the Pacific expedition, and to send him to the Burr trial belie his 1814 statement regarding Lewis's "hypochondriac affections" and his tendency to abuse alcohol.

Stephen Ambrose accents the inconsistency between Jefferson's trust in Lewis and Jefferson's 1814 statement. In his introduction to the 1988 reprint of Richard Dillon's book, Ambrose described it as a "model biography" and then referred to the significance of Jefferson's choice of Lewis to hold important positions. Ambrose wrote: "But the fact that Jefferson selected Lewis as his private secretary and dinner companion, and then to lead the expedition to explore the Louisiana Purchase, tells more about Lewis than anything I could write."[21] It is high irony, indeed, for Ambrose—who loudly and repeatedly proclaimed that Lewis killed himself—to call attention to the discrepancy between Jefferson's earlier actions and his words years later.

Virtually all historians agree that the Lewis and Clark Expedition was the culmination of Jefferson's lifelong curiosity about and fascination with the West. Surely he would not choose a person with a history of mental problems—a manic-depressive alcoholic, as some have painted Lewis—to lead such an expedition and to govern such a critically important territory. Jefferson was aging; acceptance of suicide was a "clean" way to handle the situation. Every hour of every day an official somewhere in the United States is labeling a homicide a suicide because it is the cleanest, easiest decision. So might have Jefferson.

Pulitzer Prize–winning historian Joseph Ellis in his 1997 book *American Sphinx: The Character of Thomas Jefferson* not only emphasized Jefferson's pragmatism but suggested that Jefferson had a talent for self-deception. Only four years later, David McCullough, in his masterful *John Adams* (also a Pulitzer Prize winner) demonstrated that Jefferson was capable of deception of others as well. In light of recent scholarship, how can one accept as indisputable Jefferson's statements about Lewis after his death?

No one can ever deny Jefferson's brilliance and his immeasurable contribution to the establishment of our nation, nor should they. But just because Jefferson alleged that the Lewis family had a particular medical history does not prove they did. Just because the former president accepted suicide does not prove Lewis was not murdered. While it is not unusual today for historians to attack Jefferson, some of Vardis Fisher's colleagues criticized him when he questioned some of Jefferson's character traits over four decades ago.

Retired physician William Anderson of Williamsburg, Virginia, whom I first met at the 1996 coroner's inquest, is Lewis's great-great-great-nephew. In an exchange of e-mails I asked him to explain Jefferson's remark about the family's disposition to mental problems. After reciting a family medical history, which did not include insanity, Dr. Anderson wrote, "I believe that Thomas Jefferson's assertion regarding the family was made in an effort to comfort himself by finding a scientific explanation for the news he had received from others and which he had assumed to be fact. Jefferson was human, like all of us, and he needed to explain things, and, of course, he had known the Lewis family and he was bound to have seen some of them when they were 'blue,' down, or discouraged. What better conclusion to satisfy his own mind, than to say Lewis could not help himself because he had bad genes for which he was not responsible."[22] Dr. Anderson's opinion fits perfectly into recent research on memory, reported in the 16 July 2001 issue of *Newsweek,* that indicates that memories are often illusions and that we tend to remember things as we want them to be. A simpler explanation of the discrepancy between Jefferson's earlier actions and his later statements may be that Jefferson's memory may well have been deceiving him.[23]

In the minds of many who are convinced that Lewis took his own life, the letters of William Clark constitute a determining factor in their position. James J. Holmberg in his excellent book, *Dear Brother: Letters of William Clark to Jonathan Clark,* as well as in the preceding chapter of this volume, argues vehemently that recently discovered letters offer conclusive proof of suicide. His position has merit only if one accepts—

as did Clark—the validity of contemporary reports that Lewis committed suicide. The letters of Clark and other correspondents who wrote in the immediate aftermath of Lewis's death must be understood in the context of the numerous rumors that swirled through the frontier press at that time—some of dubious origin such as those of razor slashes on the governor's arms—as well as in the context of virulent St. Louis politics. One wonders how Clark would have reacted had the report referred to a murder instead of a suicide. This is an important question that takes us right back to Priscilla Grinder and James Neelly. It is also important to keep in mind that neither Clark nor former president Jefferson had the authority to mount or demand an investigation into a crime committed in the wilderness of Tennessee, even had they been desirous of doing so.

Indeed, if one begins with the premise that we do not know how the governor died, there are alternative interpretations to Clark's letter of 28 October 1809, especially in light of the pressures Lewis faced as he attempted to govern a territory that bordered on being ungovernable. It is virtually impossible for us today to appreciate the economic, political, and social climate of St. Louis in 1809. Despite the intensity of the situation, Clark definitely expected Lewis to return to St. Louis, and in addition he expressed confidence Governor Lewis would be vindicated—hardly the views of a friend worried that his longtime companion was on the verge of a mental breakdown or suicide. In a letter to his brother two months earlier, on 26 August 1809, Clark wrote, "I think all will be right and he will return with flying Colours to this Country . . . and all he has done will Come out to be much to his Credit—as I am fully purswaded."[24] Though William Clark eventually may have believed that Lewis did kill himself, it is interesting that during a relatively long life span of sixty-eight years he did not write more about his dear friend's demise. Had he truly reconciled himself to Lewis's self-destruction, it seems natural that William Clark at some point would have expressed these convictions. In his 2004 biography of Clark, William Foley does not reveal that Clark ever addressed this issue except immediately following Lewis's death.[25]

Indeed, one wonders if William Clark in his later years did not discuss the possibility, or even the probability, of murder with his immediate family. Not long after his father's death, Meriwether Lewis Clark in his correspondence with a Tennessee clergyman inquired about reports that John Pernier had murdered Governor Lewis. He wanted to know if the Tennessee native had heard that "Lewis did not destroy his own life, but was murdered by his servant, a Frenchman, who stole his money and horses and returned to Natchez and was never heard of?"[26] Authors of a recent article suggest that it is possible William Clark's son had a hand in the movement to examine afresh the issue of how Governor Lewis died—a movement that resulted in the erection of the monument in 1848.[27] Reliance on a single letter written by William Clark immediately upon the report of suicide is not conclusive proof that Clark was convinced that Lewis killed himself.

Historians who conclude that undoubtedly Lewis shot himself seldom fail to view this journal entry on 18 August 1805—Lewis's thirty-first birthday—as evidence that he was a good candidate for suicide.

> This day I completed my thirty first year, and conceived that I had in all human probability now existed about half the period which I am to remain in this sublunary world. I reflected that I had yet done but little, very little indeed, to further the happiness of the human race, or to advance the information of the succeeding generation. I viewed with regret the many hours I have spent in indolence, and now soarly feel the want of that information which those hours would have given me had they been judiciously expended. [B]ut since they are past and cannot be recalled, I dash from me the gloomy thought and resolved in future, to redouble my exertions and at least indeavour to promote those two primary objects of human existence, by giving them the aid of that portion of talents which nature and fortune have bestowed on me; or in future, to live for mankind, as I have heretofore lived for myself.[28]

(See Document 1 for full text of the journal entry.) Stephen Ambrose, for instance, sees depression in those lines; so does Clay Jenkinson, who finds melancholia in numerous other entries as well. The citation of Lewis's birthday musings as evidence of depression provides a perfect example of what some historians call "the search for the salient quote."

Interpretation of those lines as evidence of suicidal tenancies is far-fetched, to say the least, unless one starts with the premise of suicide. Several years ago I began showing a transcription of the birthday entry to small groups of acquaintances without identifying the source, and not one person associated it with impending suicide. Then for several semesters I handed out the transcription on the first day of class to my university students with the following instructions: "Please read the selection below that was written in the early nineteenth century. Then write a few sentences about what this entry tells you about the person who wrote it." Of the several hundred paragraphs that I received over two years, not one student identified the birthday thoughts as evidence of depression or impending self-destruction. Of course, the students approached their responses from many directions, but they generally attributed positive characteristics to the author of the selection, such as intelligence, sensitivity, humanity, unselfishness, and forward thinking. Indeed, one wonders how many readers of this book have not entertained thoughts similar to those of Lewis as they approached what they considered to be the middle of their lives.

In addition to pointing to his thirty-first birthday entry, many advocates of suicide suggest that the long periods during which Lewis did not keep a journal are indicators of depression. The more one ponders the absence of Lewis's entries, the more possible explanations one can imagine. So-called writer's block generally tops the list. Even though Lewis is widely recognized as the more fluent and gracious writer of the co-captains, perhaps Clark was content with the assignment of keeping the journal. Foley, in his biography of Clark, emphasized the letter-writing proclivities of Clark and his immediate family and described him as a "practiced journal keeper" by the time the expedition began. Indeed, Foley asserted that it was "no mere happenstance that his systematic writings provided a more complete record" than those of Lewis.[29] Attributing the missing journal entries to depression is just another example of searching for support of a supposition. Where is the hard evidence that Lewis suffered from depression?

Another issue in the suicide-or-murder debate relates to the safety of the Natchez Trace. How dangerous a trip did Lewis undertake? Was an attack by bandits a distinct possibility? Or even a probability? Over the last forty years, advocates of the suicide theory have invariably cited a 1956 article by Dawson Phelps in the *William and Mary Quarterly*. Phelps described the Natchez Trace as "the most heavily traveled road of the Old Southwest" and claimed that "it was not, in 1809, a dangerous road." He pointed out that "the mail passed over it regularly."[30] Because Phelps was a veteran Park Service historian assigned to the Natchez Trace Parkway, colleagues placed a lot of weight on his assertion.

Yes, by 1809 the trace was not as dangerous as it was just a few years earlier when "Big Harpe" and "Little Harpe"—Micajah and Wiley

Harpe—and others of their ilk terrorized travelers.[31] Yes, post riders on fast horses did deliver the mail over the trace, but interestingly enough, outlaws afforded them safe passage. The most famous of the post riders was John Lee Swaney, who took ten to fifteen days to deliver mail from Nashville to Natchez or vice versa. Phelps gives one the idea that travelers frequently encountered these woodlands pony express riders. Such was not the case in 1809. Besides, the most dreaded outlaws established relationships with Swaney and often sought news of their escapades from him.[32] In her novel *The Robber Bridegroom,* Eudora Welty wrote about the irony of safe passage for postal riders.

The trace was still so dangerous in 1809, however, that the rough, tough boatmen always rode or walked up it in convoy. Travelers seldom ventured down the trace from Nashville to Natchez alone. Friends advised Alexander Wilson not to travel that trail alone, and so he rode well armed. "I had a loaded pistol in each pocket, a loaded musket belted across my shoulder, a pound of gunpowder in my flask, and five pound of shot in my belt."[33] Two years earlier, Lewis had reason to arm himself just as heavily. And he knew that. Recall that, before he settled in on the night before his death, he inquired about his gunpowder.

Furthermore, if the trace was so safe, why was Priscilla Grinder so fearful of the traveler? After all, she grew up on one of the most violent frontiers east of the Mississippi.[34]

It is also important to point out that Dawson Phelps approached his oft-cited essay with an ax to grind. That ax was his overstatement of the safety of the Natchez Trace, a position encouraged by his close association with Duke University professor William B. Hamilton. Hamilton, a native Mississippian, and Phelps were both members of the Mississippi Historical Society, and both had cause to counter the highly fictionalized account of violence on the Natchez Trace developed by Robert Coates in his 1930 best-seller, *The Outlaw Years.*

Some critics suggest that Coates, a novelist, was simply satirizing Frederick Jackson Turner's famous "frontier thesis."[35] In his 1938 Ph.D. dissertation, Hamilton openly poked fun at Turner, denying that his thesis applied to the southern frontier.[36] On the other hand, historians who did not view Coates's best-seller as satire felt his book promoted Turner's ideas. In their minds Coates may have exaggerated the violence on the trace, and Hamilton and Phelps overreacted in the other direction. In any event, for travelers of the trace as late as 1809, robbery was still a distinct possibility. Undoubtedly, Governor Lewis recognized that outlaws would view someone like himself—a gentleman traveling in the company of servants, carrying considerable luggage—an ideal target.

On another front, it has been claimed in the past decade that Meriwether Lewis killed himself while suffering from the tortures of the tertiary effects of syphilis. The claim has generated considerable attention. In a 1994 article, epidemiologist Dr. Reimert Ravenholt asserted that Lewis, on the night of 13–14 August 1805, celebrated his initial encounter with the Shoshones by accepting sexual favors offered him, and as a result he contracted syphilis.[37] While little is known regarding the sexual relations of the co-captains with Indian women, such activities by the enlisted men are well documented in the journals.[38] Indeed, several of them contracted and were treated for syphilis by Lewis with medications purchased in anticipation of their need.

As one might expect, there is no reference in the journals to either Lewis's or Clark's frolicking with the Indian women, but over the years several mixed-bloods have claimed kinship with Clark. Recently researchers discovered a baptismal record of a Joseph DeSomet Lewis who in 1872 at age sixty-eight listed Captain Meriwether Lewis as his father.[39] So the possibility exists that both co-captains could have contracted syphilis. Nevertheless, Ravenholt's theory—from his selection of the date and place of Lewis's contraction of the disease to evidence he cites to indicate that he definitely was infected—is highly speculative. Many medical experts agree that it is unlikely that in the short span of four years Lewis would have suffered from the final effects of syphilis.

The late Dr. E. G. Chuinard, professor of orthopedic surgery at the University of Oregon Medical School, mounted one of the strongest challenges to the credibility of Priscilla Grinder's account, the cornerstone of the suicide position. Dr. Chuinard asked this question: Could Lewis, if wounded as Mrs. Grinder reported, physically have staggered around her premises as she claimed to have witnessed? His answer was a resounding No! "As a surgeon, I do not believe that Lewis could have sustained the second and fatal shot with the injury to his vital organs, and live for two hours and do all the moving about related by Mrs. Grinder."[40] Chuinard also asked, even if Lewis could do all the things Grinder supposedly saw and heard—which Chuinard viewed as a physical impossibility—and if he was so intent on self-destruction, why didn't he reload his pistol or rifle and shoot himself again? Past president of the Lewis and Clark Trail Heritage Foundation and founder of its journal, Chuinard contended that Lewis suffered from malaria, and he painted a

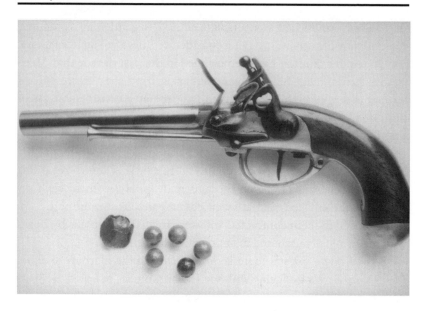

*1799 North and Cheney horseman's pistol, .69 caliber flintlock. It is widely held that this pistol, 14½ inches in overall length, is the type carried by Meriwether Lewis at the time of his death. Courtesy Professor James E. Starrs, George Washington University.*

scenario for murder at the hands of James Neelly.[41] Other medical experts agree with Chuinard that Lewis probably suffered from malaria, not only because of his symptoms but because of the drugs that he purchased in St. Louis.

Everyone seriously interested in pursuing the controversy over the manner of Lewis's death should study this superbly researched analysis by Chuinard, a proven scholar as well as a surgeon.[42] His rebuttal of the writings of Paul Cutright, Donald Jackson, and Dawson Phelps are quite useful, as are his observations regarding the positions of Vardis Fisher. Even if one questions or rejects his assertion that Neelly killed Lewis, Chuinard outlined a strong case that someone murdered Governor Lewis.

Many others question the ability of anyone to shoot himself twice with the type of pistols that Lewis carried. Most likely the pair were matched 1799 North and Cheney .69 caliber flintlocks, often known as horseman's pistols.[43] From outside of the grip to the muzzle they were

*.69 calibre pistol balls. As one observer wrote regarding someone shooting himself twice with such heavy projectiles, "the learning curve from this type of self-abuse would be quite nearly vertical." Photography courtesy of Mark Gunn, Meridian, Mississippi.*

14½ inches long. Hence, it would have been extremely difficult for one to shoot himself first in the head and then in the breast with the bullet taking a downward path before exiting low in the back. The idea of anyone shooting himself twice with such heavy pistol balls is difficult to fathom.

In 1998 a California gunsmith wrote me to find out what kind of pistols Lewis carried. After I informed him that they were most probably .69 caliber North and Cheney horseman's pistols, he quickly replied as follows:

> Received with great interest your information on the firearms used in the alleged suicide of Capt. Meryweather [sic] Lewis. Please find enclosed a pair of .69 caliber musket balls; made fresh just for you. Each ball weighs 568 GR, or 1⅓ oz; quite a heavy projectile for a handgun. No ballistic data on the North and Cheney was readily available to me, but I would guess the muzzle velocity of such a weapon to be something near 600 feet per second. At this velocity, the .69 cal. roundball would have a strik-

ing energy of 454 footpounds. Personally I am doubtful that anyone could shoot himself twice with such a weapon as *the learning curve from this type of self-abuse would be quite nearly vertical* [italics added]. Well, keep up the good work.[44]

This chap may have misspelled Meriwether, but he definitely understands the devastation inflicted upon a human body by such firepower. Historians who ultimately build their entire case upon Grinder's and Neelly's reports conveniently avoid this evidence.

Until quite recently no researcher has considered the relevance of the phase of the moon to the inquiry into the manner of Lewis's death. Several years ago a faculty colleague asserted that Mrs. Grinder could not have seen Lewis outside her cabin if there had been a new moon on the fateful night of 10–11 October 1809. Astronomical records verify that there was a new moon at 1:30 A.M. on 9 October 1809. On Tuesday, 10 October, the moon was "a waxing crescent with 3% of the Moon's visible disk illuminated." Moonset was 6:21 P.M.[45] In other words, on the heavily forested, highly humid Natchez Trace it was pitch-black the night that Lewis died. Mrs. Grinder could not have seen Lewis walking around her yard as she related to Alexander Wilson. Likewise an armed robber would have difficulty shooting his victim, even at close range.

Residents of the Great Plains or Rocky Mountains may contend that persons accustomed to the outdoors can see fairly well by starlight. And that may be the case in those regions where the stars do appear to shine more brightly. Persons who have traveled or lived on the Great Plains and in the Rockies undoubtedly have noticed how bright the stars appear. On the other hand, such is not the case along the Natchez Trace. Utter darkness prevails in that region beneath a forested canopy where the atmosphere is heavily laden with particulate matter. "Impenetrable darkness" is the way Wilson described the night along the banks of the Tennessee River.[46] It is not unusual along the trace for the humidity—water particles in the atmosphere—to run as high as the temperature. There is also the dew point to consider. Blackness prevails in the absence of moonlight or firelight where Lewis died.

After studying Alexander Wilson's account, readers will note that Priscilla Grinder described the scene in considerable detail, but she did not mention supplying a lamp or candle in the crude log cabin where the visitor slept. We know from accounts of travelers that accommodations in these stands in 1809 were extremely crude. Many preferred to sleep outside unless the weather was too inclement. Mrs. Grinder does not refer to a campfire or other type of illumination in her yard. According to Wilson's account, Lewis remarked, "Madam this is a very pleasant evening," and later observed what a "sweet evening" it was. Because days in October on the trace can be quite hot, he most likely referred to a cool evening. Perhaps he felt a gentle breeze.

The absence of moonlight opens up a whole new set of questions regarding the credibility of Mrs. Grinder as well as of Neelly, questions that add a whole new dimension to the debate. Was Grinder telling the truth? Did she concoct the story about Lewis wandering around between the guest cabin and the kitchen cabin? Chuinard implied she did. So have others. Neelly obviously knew that the moon was not shining the night of the fatal shots. It is fair to assume that Grinder told Neelly the same story reported by Wilson. If so, why did Neelly not question how she could have seen such behavior on the part of the wounded man? Why did he not raise this question in his letter to Jefferson? Maybe Vardis Fisher's description of Neelly as a shady character was on target? The late Dr. Chuinard might smile and suggest that the absence of moonlight explains why Neelly, even at point-blank range, had to shoot his victim twice.

For generations many Tennesseans who resided in the vicinity of Grinder's Stand placed credence in the lore that someone murdered Lewis. Nevertheless, for nearly half a century historians tended to accept the report of suicide. But then a legislative committee report in 1848 piqued the curiosity of national as well as local historians, who began paying attention to the question of suicide or murder. When the Tennessee legislature voted in 1848 to erect a monument in honor of Lewis, it named a committee to oversee its design and construction. In the process, they disinterred Lewis's remains and buried them beneath the monument at the site of Grinder's Stand in what is today Lewis County near the town of Hohenwald.

The committee went to great lengths to ascertain the exact location of Lewis's grave, and to avoid any error, they opened the coffin and examined the upper portion of the skeleton. After identifying and examining the remains of Lewis, the 1848 Monument Committee wrote in its report to the legislature: "The impression has long prevailed that under the influence of disease of body and mind Governor Lewis perished by his own hands. It seems to be more probable that he died by the hands of an assassin."[47] Because the committee included Dr. Samuel B. Moore,

an experienced and highly respected physician, its conclusion that someone killed Lewis must not be disregarded. It is curious that some writers,
while disdaining murder conspiracy theories, speculate that the monument committee conspired to promote the concept of death by an assailant. Of course, it is unfortunate the committee failed to reveal the precise
evidence that prompted them to issue such a bold statement. Their clear
message was "someone shot the governor." Did the doctor observe
something that precluded suicide? Perhaps he recognized bullet-caused
damage to the skeleton. One can only speculate. However, scientists
who testified at the 1996 Hohenwald coroner's inquest indicated that
sufficient evidence probably existed for an experienced and knowledgeable observer to reach such a conclusion. Indeed, his grave even today
might contain considerable forensic evidence.

This topic provides a fascinating study in historiography precisely
because those entering the fray seem to bring with them preconceived
notions, often instilled by their mentors. This is particularly true in
reactions to Vardis Fisher's 1962 book, *Suicide or Murder?* And these
predispositions or prejudices persist. Despite the depth of Fisher's research and the intriguing nature of his book, many historians continue
to view Dawson Phelps's article, rather than Fisher's book, as the authoritative statement. Phelps concludes: "In the absence of direct and
pertinent contemporary evidence to the contrary, of which not a scintilla exists, the verdict of suicide must stand."[48] What a curious line of
reasoning: Because we cannot prove murder, he must have killed himself. Why not turn that around? Because we can not prove suicide,
someone must have murdered him. Poor forensics. Worse history.

The *William and Mary Quarterly* refused to print Grace Lewis Miller's well-written thirty-six-page typescript rebuttal to the Phelps piece,
despite the fact that her missive was researched equally as well, if not better, and contained more primary sources.[49] Miller, born in St. Louis in
1895, claimed no relationship to Meriwether Lewis. After her physician-
husband died in 1935, she earned an M.A. from the University of Texas,
but though she finished requisite courses, she did not complete the
doctorate. For over three decades, beginning in the late 1930s, Miller
collected copies of manuscripts relating to the life of Meriwether Lewis,
concentrating much of her research on his postexpedition life. However,
she never did write the planned biography.

Miller was a subject of the correspondence of Fisher, Jackson, and
Phelps. She was an enigma to Fisher; to Phelps she was a joke. Jackson

showed little respect for her. "She is capable of objectivity only when Lewis's 'honor' is not at stake, I believe. She uses facts like chunks of marble to build the man a shrine, rejecting or ignoring anything that won't do for the purpose."[50] Miller, on the other hand, accused Phelps of "studied selectivity" and of citing "only such details as bear favorably on the suicide theory."[51] If her letter to the *William and Mary Quarterly*, which was never published, is representative of her scholarship, Jackson's opinion appears baseless.

Obviously, space does not permit even a summary of Miller's lengthy letter, but some of her most significant analysis related to the widespread knowledge that Lewis had suffered from malaria since his return to St. Louis in 1808. She documented the remedies upon which he frequently relied. She cited the following line from the obituary published 2 November 1809 in the *Missouri Gazette*: "The Governor has been of late very much afflicted with the fever which never failed of depriving him of his reason."[52]

Miller took Phelps to task for his lack of knowledge of Lewis's administrative accomplishments and his considerable financial assets, particularly in land holdings around the country. She labeled as "fictitious" Phelps's statement that the governor "plunged into land speculation." Miller then composed twelve pages regarding Lewis's finances. Her letter made it clear that the numerous historians who described him as insolvent erred because they failed to delve into the sources. As she concluded, "In fact, Lewis had much to live for."

Miller, as well as Vardis Fisher, made much of one of the key mysteries surrounding the death of Governor Lewis. What happened to the money? Why do so few writers mention that his wallet and its contents disappeared? By Miller's calculation, in terms of 1956 dollars, Lewis had seven hundred dollars in cash and a check worth six hundred dollars (if it had been endorsed and was negotiable). Miller asked: "Who took the money?" Her answer: "Probably Neely [*sic*] and the proprietor of Grinder's Stand both knew the answer." Like Fisher, Miller viewed Neely as a most untrustworthy character, to say the least. After all, he kept Lewis's horse, rifle, dirk, and pistols, which in itself would cast suspicion on him. In fact, Miller suspected Neely might have been a conspirator in Lewis's murder.[53]

One wonders why Fisher's *Suicide or Murder?* was not taken more seriously by historians of the American West. Anyone who studies the book carefully and who delves into the Vardis Fisher Papers at Yale University must admit that Fisher was a meticulous, diligent researcher—a man of great integrity and insatiable curiosity. Though he admitted that he could not prove murder, Fisher cast considerable doubt on evidence for suicide and presented a long list of possible suspects. So why is his stock not higher? First of all, he made his mark as a prolific and highly popular Western novelist; his doctorate from the University of Chicago was in literature, not history. Perhaps a better explanation relates to his alienation of Julian Boyd and Donald Jackson—giants in the historical profession. It is easier to understand how he offended Boyd than Jackson.

Boyd, a Princeton historian who for years edited the *Papers of Thomas Jefferson*, took offense at the manner in which Fisher quoted him. While he did not state so in his correspondence, Boyd probably was antagonized by Fisher's harsh criticism of Jefferson in *Suicide or Murder?* In the lengthy opening sentence of his chapter on Jefferson, Fisher wrote that Jefferson "has been placed by a host of image-makers on a plane above suspicion and criticism." Then Fisher asked his readers "to observe how many of the writers have accepted Jefferson's view, not only without question but almost with a bow of reverence."[54] Another line, in addition to specific criticisms of Jefferson, that must have galled Boyd read, "Having taken this great man off his pedestal and looked at a few of his frailties, and his failure of memory in his old age, we are in a better position to determine how dependable he was as a witness."[55] Today we are accustomed to scholars like Joseph Ellis and David McCullough pointing out Jefferson's weaknesses, but Fisher dared to write those words over four decades ago, when historians rarely offered such negative commentary.

Even before publication of Fisher's book, the exchange of correspondence between him and Boyd pertaining to Fisher's efforts to uncover Jefferson memoranda regarding Pernier was not exactly cordial. It became quite heated, however, after Boyd fired off a blistering letter on 26 April 1963 in which he challenged Fisher's academic integrity and even his honor. "Now, looking at the note appended to your Chapter 5, in which I am unwarrantably [*sic*] associated with your extraordinary analysis of evidence, I begin to wonder about something even more important than civility—about honor."[56]

Fisher immediately requested that James Babb, Yale librarian, return all his correspondence with Boyd. After thereby satisfying himself that he had not misrepresented Boyd, Fisher defended his statements.

Then he unloaded. "What I suspect, my dear Sir, is that you have an idolatrous attitude toward Jefferson, that my book disturbed; or that you liked to feel that Jefferson had settled the matter and that nobody less than a Jefferson scholar had a right to raise it; or that you feel you have right of preemption in the Jefferson domain and resent intrusions."[57]

More difficult to understand are the comments of Donald Jackson, published long after Fisher's death in 1968. Their exchange of numerous letters regarding research for *Suicide or Murder?* and the original manuscript had a warm, friendly—even chummy—tone.[58] On 3 August 1960, after reading his manuscript twice, Jackson wrote Fisher a friendly critique of over seven single-spaced pages. "First," Jackson assured Fisher, "I am fascinated by the thoroughness of your research and the expertness with which you have ferreted out material where I have supposed none existed." Toward the end of the letter he wrote, "You have convinced me that Neelly probably was a dishonest man and that Mrs. Grinder was a real nut." Then he added, "I am positive that you've got a good book here." His last sentence read, "But I think you owe it to our mutual friend, Meriwether Lewis, to see this thing through."[59]

To be sure, Jackson had a host of criticisms and suggestions, which stand as a tribute to his perception and insightfulness. At the top of his list was a lecture on mental illness and suicide. He wrote in part, "Certainly nobody condones suicide, but it is possible to believe that an admirable, courageous man can commit it under certain conditions. . . . For if Lewis *did* kill himself, how are you and your readers going to salvage any respect for the man?"

But Jackson's later published criticism was quite harsh. In his 1978 edition of *Letters of the Lewis and Clark Expedition*, he described Fisher's book as "verbose and inexact" and accused him of approaching "the subject not in the manner of a historian but like a detective following a very cold trail."[60] Again, in his 1987 anthology, *Among the Sleeping Giants*, Jackson took Fisher to task for writing as a "storyteller" rather than as an historian. His criticisms included allusions to Fisher's "manipulation of evidence," "reliance on oral tradition," and "emphasis on negative evidence." Jackson repeated his "detective" imagery.[61] Not all researchers agree with the validity of these charges. His reference to reliance on negative evidence is particularly curious in light of the logic applied by Phelps, whose work Jackson praised. Such harsh words are mystifying in light of the warmth and friendliness of their extensive correspondence before publication of the book. Because no historian of his generation even approached his prominence among Lewis and Clark scholars, Jackson's denigration of Fisher's work and praise for the Phelps article explain why so many historians of the American West place little credibility in Fisher's book.[62] Indeed, a surprising number of my distinguished colleagues will not even consider the possibility of homicide.[63]

Jackson's considerable impact is cited as only one example of the perpetuation and persistence of the suicide interpretation in historiography. Those whom Jackson influenced in turn have left a lasting imprint on their students, younger colleagues, and readers. Stephen Ambrose, whose *Undaunted Courage* has sold millions of copies, has done far more than any other single writer to convince Americans that Lewis killed himself. One wonders if Ambrose's preoccupation with Lewis's alleged depression, and his declaration that Lewis died by his own hand, is not explained by Ambrose's first wife's suicide, which he discusses in his moving best seller *To America: Personal Reflections of an Historian*. Regardless of the source of his views, Ambrose left a deep and indelible imprint on the historiography surrounding the death of Lewis. Consequently, it is not unusual today to see historians like William Foley, in his Clark biography, refer definitively to Lewis's death as a suicide.[64]

Certainly one should not denigrate colleagues for having firm convictions, but should they impede the search by forensic scientists for hard evidence that might preclude the possibility of suicide? There is a distinct possibility that a forensic examination of Lewis's remains could answer the question of homicide or suicide. That question ought to be answered. The identity of the assassin is, in a large sense, not as important as the determination of how he died.

The National Park Service passed up a golden opportunity after the 1996 coroner's inquest in Lewis County. The jury recommended that Lewis's remains be exhumed for the purpose of a forensic examination. However, though a petition for exhumation was filed, the case was removed to the federal court. The Park Service prevailed in the federal court, and the forensic examination was denied. A detailed account of all the legal applications and actions would take several long paragraphs; the bottom line is that the Park Service denied the request of Lewis family members for the exhumation of Lewis's remains, an act that constituted a grave disservice to American history. This is curious behavior, indeed, for a federal agency charged with protecting the nation's heritage. (It is high irony that, shortly after the Park Service denied the exhumation, the monument over Lewis's grave was completely disassembled and refurbished, and in the process workers dug to within approximately a yard of his remains.)[65]

To support its decision, the Park Service solicited letters from authors known to consider suicide as a fact—colleagues who stated in so many words that no historians of any significance any longer advocated the homicide theory.[66] Ambrose was the most succinct: "There is no question among the scholarly community—Lewis committed suicide." In effect, the Park Service ignored a host of eminent scholars who leaned heavily toward murder, including E. G. Chuinard, Elliott Coues, Reuben Thwaites, John Bakeless, Olin Wheeler, and Richard Dillon.

Dillon, whose biography Ambrose praised so highly, admitted that there is no proof of homicide and that under the right circumstances anyone can commit suicide. Nevertheless, he was adamant in his conviction that someone murdered Lewis. Here are parts of Dillon's rhetorical dialogue:

> Was Meriwether Lewis murdered? Yes. Is there proof of his murder? No. Could Lewis's death have been a suicide? Yes. . . . Is it likely that the cause of Lewis's death was self-murder? Not at all. If there is such a person as the anti-suicide type, it was Meriwether Lewis. By temperament, he was a fighter, not a quitter. Much has been made of his introspection but a line-by-line analysis of his long journals and letters show[s] his thirty-first birthday reveries (always pounced upon by suicide theorists) to be an almost unique example of moody soul-searching or excessive introspection. Sensitive he was; neurotic he was not. Lewis was one of the most positive personalities in American history.[67]

While some experts on suicide disagree with Dillon, others support his analysis of Lewis's personality. After performing a "psychological autopsy" on Lewis, criminal psychologist Dr. Thomas Steed testified at the Hohenwald inquest that Lewis was not suicidal.[68]

If someone murdered Lewis, obviously the next question is, Who? Chuinard is not alone in targeting James Neelly, but John Pernier is another frequently mentioned suspect. So is Robert Grinder, owner of the stand, either alone or in connivance with his wife, Priscilla. Most proponents of murder view Neelly, Pernier, and Robert Grinder as the most likely perpetrators. However, a couple of years ago one of my students, after I read a paper on this topic, said: "Dr. Guice, it is pretty simple; Lewis came on too strong to Mrs. Grinder and she shot him!" Could be. More likely it was an unknown assailant.

Several authors have suggested that Lewis was the victim of a conspiracy. In 1962 Jonathan Daniels wrote, "But if Lewis was murdered, as good a guess as any is that Wilkinson ordered it, Bates arranged it, Pernia [*sic*] did it."[69] Others have suggested a similar scenario, with Neelly as the assassin because General Wilkinson was his ultimate military commander. For the same reasons, some include Russell in the conspiracy.

Most historians consider the conspiracy theory offered in 1994 by David Leon Chandler rather far-fetched, but his reasons for General Wilkinson's participation have some appeal.[70] According to Chandler, Wilkinson planned and arranged for the assassination of Lewis and Thomas Jefferson covered it. While Jefferson's 1814 remembrances provide only the weakest kind of evidence for suicide, it is impossible to believe that Jefferson conspired with Wilkinson to eliminate Lewis. Wilkinson, on the other hand—one of the shadiest characters in the history of the United States—had ample reasons to want Lewis removed from his powerful position in St. Louis.

Murder was not only a possibility, but a probability.[71] Unfortunately, only a forensic examination of the remains can prove homicide. Hopefully, the Park Service will soon allow that to happen. Meanwhile, this historian of the Natchez Trace finds it incredible—even inconceivable— that any scholar would dare state *unequivocally* that Meriwether Lewis contemplated suicide as he rode into Grinder's Stand that pleasant fall evening in 1809. A perfect target for outlaws, Lewis was probably their victim.

## Notes

1. Clark and Guice, *Old Southwest.*
2. Jackson, *Letters,* 2:591–92.
3. Holmberg, *Dear Brother,* 206–28.
4. Kushner, "Suicide," 464–81.
5. Phelps, "Tragic Death," 305–18.
6. Ravenholt, "Triumph Then Despair," 366–79.
7. For a detailed treatment of Lewis's 1807 activities in Philadelphia, see Cutright, "Contributions," 21–29.
8. Jackson, *Letters,* 2:728.

9. Dillon, *Meriwether Lewis* (1965), 288.

10. Ibid., 290

11. Colter-Frick, "Meriwether Lewis's Personal Finances," 16–20; Miller, letter of 16 December 1966, Grace Lewis Miller Papers.

12. Jackson, *Letters*, 2:464–65.

13. Ibid., 466–67.

14. *Coroner's Inquest*, 216–17.

15. Ibid., 573–75.

16. Ibid., 223–25.

17. Ibid., 274–88.

18. Fisher to Jackson, 9 July 1960, Vardis Fisher Papers.

19. For a description and analysis of Fisher's book, see Guice, "Fisher and Meriwether Lewis."

20. Jackson, *Letters*, 2:467–68.

21. Ambrose, foreword to 1988 reprint of Dillon, *Meriwether* Lewis, xi–xii.

22. Anderson message of 24 May 2001.

23. Fisher, *Suicide or Murder?* 171–82. In his 1 September 1960 letter to Donald Jackson, Fisher quoted Boyd, "These Precious Moments": "It is also pertinent to observe that Jefferson, whose memory in old age caused him at times to err. . . ."

24. Holmberg, *Dear Brother*, 210.

25. Foley, *Wilderness Journey*.

26. Coues, *History*, 1:lxi.

27. Fausz and Gavin, "Death of Meriwether Lewis."

28. Moulton, *Journals*, 5:118.

29. Foley, *Wilderness Journey*, 3, 24.

30. Phelps, "Tragic Death," 317.

31. Guice, " Trace of Violence?"

32. Clark and Guice, *Old Southwest*, 94–95.

33. Alexander Wilson, "Particulars," 34–35.

34. When I first read Wilson's account of his interview with Priscilla Grinder, I found her behavior quite strange for someone reared in eastern Tennessee, which had a heritage of violence.

35. Guice, "Trace of Violence?" 137–39.

36. Hamilton, "American Beginnings."

37. Ravenholt, "Triumph Then Despair." For a summary of Ravenholt's arguments, see Guice, "Fatal Rendezvous" (1998), 9–10.

38. Ronda, *Lewis and Clark*; Tennant, "Sexual Relations."

39. Thompson, "Meriwether Lewis and His Son."

40. Chuinard, "How Did Meriwether Lewis Die?" 18:1, 6.

41. Ibid., 6, 18.

42. Chuinard, *Only One Man Died*.

43. *Coroner's Inquest*, 22–23.

44. Rodney Jay Tripp to John D. W. Guice, Santa Clarita, Calif., 1998. Tripp did not date the handwritten letter and the postmark is illegible except for the year, 1998.

45. U. S. Naval Observatory, Astronomical Applications Department, Sun and Moon Data for One Day, Tuesday, 10 October 1809, http://mach.usno.navy.mil/cgi-hin/aa_pap.pl. For a detailed discussion of this question, see Guice, "Moonlight and Meriwether Lewis."

46. Alexander Wilson, "Particulars," 41.

47. Starrs, *Meriwether Lewis*, 28–32. In particular, Starrs cites Robert White, "Report," 4:385–87, and *Tennessee Journal of the House of Representatives*, 86:238–40 and appendix.

48. Phelps, "Tragic Death," 317.

49. Miller, letter of 16 December 1966.

50. Jackson to Fisher, 16 May 1960, Fisher Papers.

51. Miller, letter of 16 December 1966.

52. Ibid.

53. Ibid. Fisher expressed puzzlement that the vast majority of writers fail to mention that Lewis's purse and money disappeared during the night. Fisher, *Suicide or Murder?* 136. John Marks, Lewis's half-brother, later recovered the horse and rifle.

54. Fisher, *Suicide or Murder?* 171.

55. Ibid., 178.

56. Boyd to Fisher, 26 April 1963, Fisher Papers.

57. Fisher to Boyd, 14 May 1963, Fisher Papers.

58. The Fisher Papers at Yale include at least six letters from Fisher to Jackson and nine from Jackson to Fisher. The inclusive dates are 10 May 1960 to 21 February 1961.

59. Jackson to Fisher, 3 August 1960, Fisher Papers. One cannot fail to see the high irony in the fact that, though ultimately the case for suicide rests on the statements of Priscilla Grinder, Jackson himself, a leading proponent of the suicide theory, labeled her "a real nut."

60. Jackson, *Letters*, 2:748

61. Jackson, *Among Sleeping Giants*, 68–70.

62. Guice, "Fisher and Meriwether Lewis."

63. For the purpose of illustration, please allow a moment of personal privilege. I vividly recall a telephone conversation with Professor James Ronda as I was preparing a proposal for a session on the death of Lewis at the 1994 annual conference of the Western History Association. When I invited him to chair the session, he declined with words to this effect: "The death of Lewis is not worthy of a session because there is no doubt that he committed suicide." Gary Moulton, to whom all American historians are indebted for his superbly edited, monumental edition of *Journals of the Lewis and Clark Expedition*, warned me that he also believes that Lewis killed himself. Nevertheless, he

graciously chaired the session that attracted one of the largest audiences of the conference. One only has to talk with Ronda or read the acknowledgments in the original edition and the introduction to the bicentennial edition of his classic *Lewis and Clark among the Indians* to understand the impact that Donald Jackson had upon Ronda's life, career, and scholarship. They truly enjoyed an admirable professional relationship—one that any historian would envy. The remarkably perceptive and prescient Jackson was indeed the "dean of Lewis and Clark scholars," and his *Letters of the Lewis and Clark Expedition* deserve Ronda's description as "magisterial."

64. Foley, *Wilderness Journey*, 165.

65. For a detailed discussion of the legal efforts to exhume Lewis's remains, see Starrs, *Voice for the Dead*, 248–71. The rededication ceremonies for the restored monument took place on 11 October 2001. *Lewis County (Tenn.) Herald*, 18 October 2001; National Park Service, Meriwether Lewis Rededication Ceremony Program, Natchez Trace Parkway, Hohenwald, Tennessee, 11 October 2001.

66. Stephen Ambrose to Barry Mackintosh, 25 August 1998; Gary Moulton to Barry Mackintosh, 16 September 1998; Gary Moulton to Robert Stanton, 22 January 1998; James Ronda to Barry Mackintosh, 5 September 1998. James Starrs obtained copies of these letters through the Freedom of Information Act.

67. Dillon, *Meriwether Lewis* (1965), 344.

68. *Coroner's Inquest*, 121–58.

69. Daniels, *Devil's Backbone*, 182.

70. Chandler, *Jefferson Conspiracies*.

71. Dillon, *Meriwether Lewis* (1965), 335–50. In an exchange of phone calls and postcards with me some twenty to twenty-five years after the original publication of his biography of Meriwether Lewis, Dillon held fast to his conviction that Lewis was murdered. Furthermore, in rather salty language he insisted that many historians started with the premise of suicide and then sought evidence to support their position. Dillon encouraged me to continue studying the topic.

# CHAPTER THREE

# A Postmortem Trial concerning Meriwether Lewis's Controversial Death

**JAY H. BUCKLEY**

On the afternoon of the second day of June 1805 in north-central Montana, the Lewis and Clark Expedition faced a defining moment when it arrived at a fork in the Missouri River. The stream flowing in from the northwest was wide and muddy, similar to the big muddy river they had ascended for the last two thousand miles. The western branch was swifter, shallower, clearer, and flowed out of the distant mountains. The Arrowsmith map and other references the captains had with them did not mention this fork in the river, nor did the information they had gathered from the Mandans and Hidatsas during the previous winter. Moreover, the sound of the Great Falls of the Missouri, which would have confirmed which one was the principal river, could not be heard.

The captains were convinced they were right in supposing that the western river was the object of their pursuit. Veteran watermen like Pierre Cruzatte and the rest of the party, however, believed the captains were in error. To make a wrong decision was unthinkable. It would cause the expedition to use up precious supplies and lose valuable time, perhaps even the entire traveling season. It would also demoralize the men, possibly threaten their lives, and could thwart the entire mission. It was time to reach the Rockies, find the Shoshones, trade for horses, portage the Continental Divide, descend the Columbia, and reach the Pacific before winter.

The captains, recognizing the importance of their decision, took extra precautions. They spent the day thinking about their decision. Lewis commented that "our cogitating faculties been busily employed all day."[1] They sent search parties up both forks and had them return and report. The results were inconclusive, prompting the captains to set out to see for themselves. Braving the rain and treacherous footing, Clark traveled nearly fifty miles up the Missouri and found that it ran to the southwest. Lewis ascended the northern branch about seventy miles and confirmed his suspicions that it ran too far north to lead to the Pacific. On 8 June 1805 Lewis wrote, "The whole of my party to a man except myself were fully peswaided that this river was the Missouri, but being fully of opinion that it was neither the main stream or that which it would be advisable for us to take, I determined to give it a name and . . . called it Maria's River."[2]

The next day, despite field observations and reconnaissance, Lewis confided in his journal, "I indevoured to impress on the minds of the party all of whom except Capt. C. being still firm in the beleif that the N. Fork was the Missouri and that which we ought to take; they said very cheerfully that they were ready to follow us any wher we thought proper to direct but that they still thought that the other was the river . . . it was agreed between Capt. C. and myself that one of us should set out with a small party by land up the South fork and continue our rout up it untill we found the falls."[3] In other words, the captains still saw the western branch as the true Missouri and the men retained their hunches that the Maria's (the modern-day Marias) was the principal stream. Nevertheless, even though many of them still felt the captains were wrong, they cached part of their supplies and equipment, packed their bags, and proceeded on. It took until mid-June before Lewis, traveling ahead on foot, arrived at the Great Falls of the Missouri and sent that welcome information back to the oncoming party to "settle in their minds all further doubts as to the Missouri."[4]

Just as the confluence of the Marias and Missouri rivers caused a difference of opinion on the Lewis and Clark Expedition, the death of the leader of the voyage has generated equal disagreement and controversy among the followers of the Lewis and Clark Trail and the tellers of the Lewis and Clark story. With so much written during the past two centuries by Lewis and Clark and about Lewis and Clark, it is amazing that the fateful ends of three of the most familiar expedition members—York, Sacagawea, and, especially, Lewis—continue to prompt debate. One would think that after two hundred years of historical research and a thorough examination of existing evidence historians would be able to put to rest discrepancies about these individuals, particularly about their deaths.

There is no controversy surrounding William Clark's death. He died on 1 September 1838 at the seasoned age of sixty-eight in St. Louis. What became of his slave, York, however, still generates some disagreements. After 1815, York's whereabouts remain unknown. Clark told Washington Irving in 1832 that he had eventually freed York and gave him a large wagon and team to operate between Nashville and Richmond. The story continued that York was unhappy, wanted to return to Clark, and eventually died of cholera in Tennessee sometime between 1816 and 1832. Nevertheless, rumors persisted that York escaped from Clark and the confines of slavery by fleeing up the Missouri, where he lived out his life in the Rocky Mountains among the Crows.[5]

Sacagawea's death elicits additional controversy. Most historians believe that she died near Fort Manuel in South Dakota on 20 December 1812. Clark listed her as deceased in an account book list he compiled in the late 1820s. He should have known, especially since he was the legal guardian of Jean-Baptiste and Lisette, the two children she had with Toussaint Charbonneau.[6] Yet oral traditions of the Comanches and Shoshones advance the possibility that she lived for decades, married a man named Jerk Meat, and had five more children before eventually dying on the Wind River Reservation in Wyoming in 1884.[7]

Unlike some of the uncertainly surrounding the death dates for York and Sacagawea, Meriwether Lewis definitely died from the effects of gunshot wounds on 11 October 1809. Since death by natural causes has been ruled out, the controversy surrounds how those bullets entered his body: by suicide, by homicide, or by accident? Why does it matter? Would understanding the manner of Lewis's death increase or diminish his life's contributions? Would proving that his death occurred by suicide wreck his reputation, indicate that he failed to adjust to postexpedition life, and overshadow his expedition exploits? Could an exhumation of Lewis's remains provide a definite answer to the cause of death and produce enough DNA evidence to support or refute the allegation that Lewis fathered a Sioux child named Joseph DeSomet Lewis?[8] If the National Park Service allowed the exhumation of Lewis's body, what precedent would it set regarding the exhumation of other famous historical figures? What about the fact that almost two hundred Lewis descendants want to exonerate the man some historians have stereotyped as a drunk, depressed, disease-ridden drug addict, a manic-depressive, a spurned suitor, and a suicidal syphilitic suffering from posttraumatic stress disorder?

In 1990 the editors of the *American Heritage* publication asked dozens of members of the Society of American Historians the following question: "What is the one mystery in United States history you would like to see resolved?" Dee Brown responded, "How Did Meriwether Lewis Die?"[9] Whether or not Lewis died by his own hand or someone else's matters to lots of folks: to Lewis's descendants who want to clear his good name; to possible relatives who want to prove a biological connection; to people residing along the Natchez Trace who take pride in the accuracy of their local history; to residents of Lewis County, Tennessee; to members of the Lewis County Historical Society; to members of the Lewis and Clark Trail Heritage Foundation; to forensic scientists who assert that exhumation could help resolve this historical dispute; to those interested in using the advantages of modern science to help solve historical mysteries; to historians interested in presenting the nation with a history written as correctly and accurately as humanly possible; and to people everywhere who simply want to know.

Perhaps the best way to uncover the truth about what really happened that October evening at Grinder's Stand is for readers to exercise their "cogitating faculties" while vicariously participating in a postmortem trial to determine whether or not Lewis's death was self-inflicted, accidental, or caused by someone else. The preceding essays have addressed the uncertainties and historical controversies surrounding his death. Did Lewis, influenced by disease of body and mind, perish by his own hand as James Holmberg contends? Or did he, as John Guice suggests, die as the result of a murder conspiracy mounted by a litany of would-be suspects or perhaps at the hands of an unknown assassin frequenting the Natchez Trace? Like the decision Lewis and Clark faced at the Marias River, readers would be well served to keep an open mind about all of the possibilities and be willing to explore the available alternatives, or even suggest new theories, before proceeding on. A fresh look at the evidence may be the only way to uncover the name of the person or persons responsible for Meriwether Lewis's mysterious and controversial death.

Exhume the body! Oh, the story those bones might tell. Should forensic scientists be able to uncover vital evidence that might shed some light on what happened that fateful October night at Grinder's Stand in Tennessee, what might they unearth? Would they find the entrance and exit wounds, signs of syphilis or malaria, the presence of black-powder residue or mercury, the lead balls that killed Lewis, or even, perhaps, a crumpled piece of paper in Lewis's hand identifying the perpetrator or culprits? Lewis's descendants and others want to add credence to the possibility that someone murdered this important American figure. What harm could be done?

There have been a host of historical figures who have suffered untimely deaths by assassination, disappearance, dueling, and murder. Exhumation should be considered only in a very select number of these cases and when descendants are willing to grant permission. Yet it is extremely rare to find an instance where suicide is suspected as the cause of death for these historical icons, as it is in the case of Lewis. Moreover, scientists have made inroads in resolving historical mysteries like Lewis's through forensic evidence. For brevity, two recent examples must suffice. Zachary Taylor was presumed to have died by arsenic poisoning. In 1991, after his descendants granted permission for exhumation of his remains from a Louisville cemetery, neutron activation analysis tests performed by Larry Robinson and Frank Dyer ruled out that possibility. For hundreds of years people believed King Tut (d. 1323 B.C.) had been murdered by a blow to the head. In 2005 the National Geographic Society released 3-D images from a CAT scan of his body that revealed what he looked like as a healthy nineteen-year-old. More important, Dr. Zahi Hawass and his team of scientists overturned the murder theory by demonstrating that Tut likely died of complications resulting from a broken left leg suffered a few days before his death. These examples show that history and science can work together in seeking truth.[10]

This would not be the first time such a request has been made. In fact, Lewis's remains may have been exhumed twice already! More than 150 years ago, the Tennessee legislature authorized a commission to exhume Lewis's grave to authenticate his remains before establishing a national monument at the site. According to the Lewis Monument Committee report, they found some bones and other items, vouched for his remains, and concluded that Lewis probably was murdered. The evidence they found to justify their conclusion, however, is unverifiable.[11] Later, a coroner's jury convened in 1996 to hear the testimony of fourteen witnesses (comprising historians, pathologists, psychiatrists, firearms experts, document examiners, and other forensic scientists) who unanimously recommended disinterment.[12]

Another exhumation request came in 1998 from George Washington University professor of law and forensic sciences James Starrs, who, as a leading scientific sleuth involved in similar controversies surrounding figures like Jesse James and John Wilkes Booth, contends that Lewis's story can best be told by his remains. Such an exhumation would not only provide skeletal clues about Lewis's death, but would also enable DNA testing to support or refute DeSomet Lewis's parentage claim.[13]

Alaska Senator Frank H. Murkowski, a former ranking member of the Senate Energy and Natural Resources Committee, made the most recent request of the National Park Service in 2002 when he asked the agency to settle the dilemma by exhuming Lewis's body. Murkowski said, "Meriwether Lewis deserves better than to be in the middle of a mystery whose solution is within reach. . . . World-class scientists are standing by ready to give his family and history the answers."[14]

Author Stephen Ambrose, Montana artist Larry Janoff, and others opposed exhumation. Janoff was "appalled that the so-called 'experts' can get away with making false and misleading statements in order to benefit possible financial gain from notoriety that a stunt such as this would generate." Moreover, he added, shortly after the first burial, "hogs got into [Lewis's grave] and unfortunately consumed much of the body." The 1848 disinterment supposedly found only "a few small bones" and "a couple of buttons."[15] Those opposed to exhuming him recommended remembering Lewis's accomplishments in life and not worrying further about the manner of his death.

The National Park Service agreed, denying the exhumation requests in 1996, 1998, and 2002 and cited as one of the reasons for denying the requests the undesirable precedent of disturbing graves not threatened by natural elements or by development. Adding to the irony is that only a short while after the Park Service denied the 1996 request, the monument over Lewis's grave was dismantled for renovation. In fact, excavation came within a few feet of any remains before the restored monument was rededicated on 11 October 2001.

Katherine Brock, interpretive specialist for the Natchez Trace Parkway, conceded that "There is no evidence to show one way or the other. . . . As the government you have to take a neutral side in it, whether you like it or not." Moreover, Brock said that there is no assurance that Lewis is even buried beneath or near the monument near Howenwald, Tennessee, noting that she had "never read anything, in the archives or otherwise, that said his body had been moved to that spot" and that the Park Service was not going to "dig [around] looking for him."[16] The manager of the Lewis and Clark National Historic Trail, Richard Williams, has also taken a pragmatic approach. "It may be better that it is a mystery. . . . That way people can choose what to believe."[17]

So, until the bones are dug up—if they ever are—and before the extant evidence is reexamined, readers must be satisfied with current findings and interpretations. As the vicarious postmortem trial begins, readers should keep in mind that there are not many hard facts or pieces of primary evidence—physical remains, eyewitness accounts, exact time of death—that would help clarify the case. As a result, the court is left with an abundance of theories, opinions, hearsay evidence, supposition, and contestable contemporary accounts, all espoused by expert and lay witnesses who fall on both sides of the debate.

To begin the postmortem trial, the prosecution alleges Lewis is guilty of self-murder, of taking his own life. The attorneys for the prosecution fully believe they have a clear-cut case and that the relevant testimony suggests suicide. James Holmberg has ably laid out the evidence, but some of it bears restating briefly, as does a review of expert testimony from modern-day authors who have weighed in on the matter. Then, John Guice and other experts will present their defense.

Readers of this essay have hereby been duly sworn in as vicarious jurors, sequestered in their homes, cars, or offices until they are asked to render a verdict.

The prosecution's opening statement retells the story of the tragic ending of one of America's greatest heroes, Meriwether Lewis, co-commander of the Lewis and Clark Expedition. Because of personal and public pressures, they argue, Lewis took his own life on the Natchez Trace in mid-October 1809. In fact, nearly all of the contemporary

*Meriwether Lewis Site, Natchez Trace Parkway. The monument commemorating Meriwether Lewis sits amid gravestones in a pioneer cemetery near Hohenwald, Tennessee. Courtesy Natchez Trace Parkway, National Park Service.*

An officer of the Regular Army. Private Secretary to President Jefferson. Commander of the Expedition to the Oregon in 1803-1806. Governor of the Territory of Louisiana. His melancholy death occurred where this monument now stands and under which rest his mortal remains.

*Meriwether Lewis Monument, Natchez Trace Parkway. This monument, erected in 1848 by the State of Tennessee, sits atop the remains of Lewis just off the Natchez Trace Parkway. Courtesy Natchez Trace Parkway, National Park Service.*

evidence concerning Lewis's setbacks and failures during his postexpedition life, the prosecution insists, points to this sad, but inevitable, conclusion. The defense, the prosecution forewarns, will posture and try to manipulate the evidence; discredit the witnesses; use negative evidence to prove the opposite; and give undue credence to oral traditions, murder theories, rumors, and reports from two coroner's juries held in 1848 and 1996, respectively.

The defense's opening remarks suggest, even beg, that the jurors keep an open mind, consider the credibility issues associated with most of the contemporary evidence they will hear, and remember that Lewis is innocent until proven guilty. The prosecution, they contend, will deliver a list of Lewis's shortcomings and will downplay his many successes—as pathfinder to the western sea, as personal secretary of Thomas Jefferson, and as governor of the Territory of Upper Louisiana. While there exists the possibility Lewis may have taken his own life, the defense concludes, enough evidence exists or remains disputed to raise reasonable doubt and even suggest he was killed by accident or murder.

The prosecution's case hinges upon the contemporary evidence that, they believe, categorically points to suicide. As James Holmberg has clearly outlined in his essay in this volume, the evidence supporting suicide fits into three general categories: first, at the time of Lewis's death, the verdict was suicide; second, all of the recorded accounts in the first few years agree on the cause of death; and third, nearly all who heard the news concurred. Finally, a litany of opinions and positions will be offered by proponents of the suicide theory. The case proceeds on.

During the summer of 1809, Lewis was a troubled man, concerned that his world was falling apart. Certainly he faced significant pressures as governor of Upper Louisiana. Not only did he lack the support of the territorial secretary, Frederick Bates, but his superiors in Washington disputed some of his expenditures and decisions. His confidence was shaken, his integrity questioned, and his credit ruined. Other difficulties resulted from his tardiness in going to St. Louis after his executive appointment and his inability to get along with many of the territorial residents once he took up his post. Lewis also apparently had difficulty adjusting to postexpedition life, failed in several attempts at courtship, and may have turned to alcohol for solace. His friend William Clark was concerned about his journey east in the fall of 1809, partly because of Lewis's ill health and partly because Lewis's mind seemed troubled about possible financial and political ruin. Lewis's mentor, Thomas Jefferson, had also chastised Lewis for not corresponding regularly and for not preparing the expedition journals for publication in a timely fashion.

In addition to these personal, political, and financial failures, the ten oral and written contemporary accounts of those who met Lewis during his last two weeks on earth—the majority of them attributed to Priscilla Grinder, James Neelly, John Pernier, and Gilbert Russell—must be considered. All supported, more or less, the claim that Lewis took his own life. Later accounts by John Brahan and Alexander Wilson, as well as the anonymous friend who wrote Lewis's obituary, all concurred with the verdict of suicide, as did William Clark and Thomas Jefferson, the two men who knew Lewis best. As Jefferson later penned, "About 3. oclock in the night he did the deed which plunged his friends into affliction and deprived his country of one of her most valued citizens."[18] Moreover, when Bates, Clark, Jefferson, and people from St. Louis to Philadelphia heard the news—either through gossip, newspaper reports, or letters—they apparently accepted the tragic details without raising any doubts to the contrary.

Bolstering all of this contemporary evidence are testimonials from modern-day experts who have weighed in over the course of the last fifty years, offering their expertise and professional opinions supporting the claim that Lewis committed suicide. A cursory examination of the witness list is impressive: Stephen Ambrose, Ken Burns, Paul Cutright, Jonathan Daniels, Thomas Danisi, Dayton Duncan, William Foley, James Holmberg, Reginald Horsman, Donald Jackson, Kay Jamison, Clay Jenkinson, Howard Kushner, Aaron Less, Ronald Loge, Boynton Merrill, John Moore, Larry Morris, Gary Moulton, David Nicandri, David Peck, Dawson Phelps, Reimert Ravenholt, James Ronda, and John Westefeld among others.

Dawson Phelps's 1956 article was among the first to lay out some of the plausible reasons why Lewis may have committed suicide. His explanations for Priscilla Grinder's interesting behavior, the assertion that the Natchez Trace was a safe place, and his conviction that Lewis suffered from depression were sufficient to convince a bevy of historians that suicide was not only likely but probable.[19] The venerable Lewis and Clark scholar Donald Jackson stated in 1962 that "I am inclined to believe that Lewis died by his own hand."[20] His pro-suicide/anti-murder opinion did much to affect a generation of scholars who held Jackson in high esteem. Other writers added their convictions as well. In 1981 Howard Kushner's psychoanalytical inquiry suggested, "[A]ny person not disturbed by the kinds of financial, political, and personal loss that Lewis suffered would be truly mad." Kushner attributed Lewis's suicide, in part, to the incomplete mourning Lewis experienced in the wake of his father's death when the boy was very young, which helped to explain Lewis's "repeated failure to establish lasting interpersonal relations, extreme risk-taking, and a compulsive desire for self-punishment.[21] Paul Cutright, too, listed the now-familiar pillars that support the suicide theories: (1) no wife; (2) depression and intemperance; (3) failure to publish; and (4) loss of Jefferson's confidence and filial support.[22]

Most recently, professors John Westefeld and Aaron Less presented another psychological perspective. They conducted a suicide assessment "to evaluate the nature of Lewis's historical, personal, psychosocial environmental, and clinical risk factors, and protective factors" and concluded that the evidence of mental illness, substance abuse, medical problems, temperament, and numerous stresses demonstrated that "Lewis was at a high suicide risk at the time of his death, and that the preponderance of the evidence indicates that he died by his own hand."[23]

Adding credibility to the suicide theory, historian and editor Gary Moulton concluded in 1986 that after Lewis became Louisiana territorial governor "he encountered difficulties that caused him severe emotional problems. He died by his own hand on the Natchez Trace in Tennessee."[24] Lewis and Clark aficionados sat up and took notice when Jackson and Moulton weighed in on the argument. Since Jackson's *Letters of the Lewis and Clark Expedition* and Moulton's *Journals of the Lewis and Clark Expedition* comprise the canon for Lewis and Clark scholarship, it is not too surprising that many authors of the last half century have adhered to their explanations as the definitive word. A decade after Moulton's declaration, Stephen Ambrose's *Undaunted Courage*, the most well-known and widely read biography of Lewis, placed the suicide theory firmly into the American mainstream, attributing Lewis's demise to a combination of debts, depression, drinking, and drug use.[25]

Clay Jenkinson's recent biography of Lewis accepted the suicide theory as well, but he expanded upon the reasoning and the context surrounding it. Jenkinson noted that Lewis was extremely busy from 1807 to 1809. Governor Lewis issued proclamations, employed a publisher for the territorial laws, helped organize the expeditions to build factories at Forts Osage and Madison, became the first Master Mason of St. Louis Lodge No. 111, orchestrated the return of the Mandan Chief Sheheke, approved Indian treaties negotiated by the Indian agents, and encouraged the efforts of the Missouri Fur Company to extend the fur trade up the Missouri. Certainly a person filled with despair could not accomplish so much. Yet, he concluded, Lewis probably was a manic-depressive, perhaps bipolar, unlucky at love, and faced pressures to get the journals published. Financial concerns over his political expenditures and opposition from his territorial secretary, Frederick Bates, in addition to all the rest on his mind, may have culminated in a self-examination of himself that did not meet his own standard and contributed to his early demise.[26]

Others have worked to find additional satisfactory explanations for suicide. In 1980, Marian White built upon the works of earlier scholars in a thorough discussion of how the effects of malaria had destroyed Lewis's health.[27] More recently, Thomas Danisi proposed that Lewis's "hypochondria" could indeed be attributed to the great pain he suffered because of the effects of malaria. Lewis did not intend to commit suicide, Danisi insisted, but in order to relieve his suffering, he accidentally wounded himself to allay his pain as "a strange and tragic form of self-surgery [caused by the malady], not suicide."[28]

Others look to moments in the expedition to find reasons they think support suicide. Seattle epidemiologist Dr. Reimert Ravenholt suggested that it was the physical and mental effects of an advanced stage of *neurosyphilis paresis*, or syphilis contracted on the expedition, that compelled Lewis to end his life. This epidemiologist took the argument one step farther by pinpointing the likely liaison with a Shoshone woman on 13 or 14 August 1805, as to when Lewis purportedly contracted the disease.[29] David Nicandri has postulated that "the first cracks in Lewis's psyche occurred in the Pacific Northwest." The physical challenges and hardships the expedition faced on the Columbia Plateau took a psychological toll on Lewis that may have led to disorders such as a weakened immune system, cyclothymia (a bipolar disorder that persists over a long time), unipolar depression, or perhaps even complex posttraumatic stress disorder.[30]

Despite all of the possible reasons—financial problems, alcoholism, addictions, failure to marry, mental illness, political pressures, depression, and the possible effects of syphilis, malaria, or posttraumatic stress disorder—the latest scholarship has returned to the statements offered by William Clark in 1809. Of Lewis's acquaintances, only Clark has never been implicated in causing or covering up Lewis's death. Clark's letters, then, offer some of the best evidence that he believed Lewis died by his own hand. Clark knew Lewis better than anyone except, perhaps, Lewis's mother, Lucy. Lewis's superior officer during Washington's Indian War in the Ohio Valley during the 1790s, Clark had then spent three years with him on the expedition sharing all of its difficulties and dangers, saw him on a daily basis in St. Louis, dined with him, lent him money, and agreed to witness the execution of his will. From the time Clark first heard the news of Lewis's death, in letter after letter to his brother thereafter, and even after visiting with Jefferson at Monticello, Clark apparently never doubted the suicide, unless it was later in his life. He, more than anyone else, would have done all in his power to investigate had he suspected anything out of the ordinary. Reading the newspaper reports that Lewis had taken his own life evoked an emotional response in Clark, and he lamented to his brother Jonathan, "I fear O! I fear the waight of his mind has over come him, what will be the Consequence?"[31]

Two hundred years later, two recent biographers of William Clark have agreed with Clark's initial assessment. "It was suicide," Landon Jones wrote: "That was the unequivocal testimony from the scene by Neely, Pernier, and Mrs. Grinder. Clark immediately came to the same conclusion, as did Jefferson."[32] William Foley likewise reached the conclusion that "Lewis was dead, from a self-inflicted gunshot wound."[33]

The jurors are left to ponder what appears as a seemingly overwhelming contemporary record supporting suicide. Moreover, little evidence suggested foul play, few newspaper reports challenged the governor's death as a suicide, few accounts deviated from this conclusion, and only a few of Lewis's friends and associates suspected murder. In the words of the Natchez Trace historian Dawson Phelps, "In the absence of direct and pertinent contemporary evidence to the contrary, of which not a scintilla exists, the verdict of suicide must stand."[34]

The prosecution rests, with Clark's lamentation echoing in the courtroom: "I fear O! I fear the waight of his mind has over come him, what will be the Consequence?"

The defense can now employ a variety of strategies to counter the suicide theory. These include discrediting the contemporary witnesses; refuting conflicting evidence surrounding the various accounts of his death; offering new evidence; naming potential murderers or accomplices; and providing experts to testify that murder is at least a possibility, if not a probability.

John Guice's essay in this volume lays the groundwork for the defense and postulates that Lewis's death was the result of foul play. Guice outlines at least sixteen reasons why some scholars favor the suicide interpretation and then tries to account for them. Lewis faced multiple pressures to publish or perish, to find and keep a wife, and to deal with some troubles at work. He had bounced a few checks and needed to rectify a bad credit report. Many academics deal with those same challenges today. What are the possible effects malaria, syphilis, and illness had on Lewis? Who has not ever been sick or depressed? It does not mean one is crazy. What about Lewis's use of alcohol and opiates to dull his senses? Even conservative talk-show host Rush Limbaugh recently admitted similar problems, and only a portion of America considered him insane. The defense contends that many of those who believe Lewis committed suicide arrive at that conclusion in advance, build their case around the evidence that seems to support it, and discount or reject out of hand additional evidence or questions that undermine their position.

Professor Guice ably presents the unexplained phenomena surrounding the case that suggest murder: Lewis's missing money and personal effects; the total darkness of that night due to the phases of the moon; a botched suicide attempt by a man skilled in using weaponry. Lewis had at least two wounds: one in the head and another in the chest from two deadly .69 caliber pistols (and, according to some accounts, razor cuts on his arms, legs, and neck). Incredibly, these wounds not only failed to kill him, but they did not even prevent him from wandering around the premises for several hours. That Lewis died of gunshot wounds is not disputed, but there were no actual witnesses to the shooting. The differing accounts of the killing were based on rumor and hearsay, and no official autopsy report was filed to provide a consistent account of the nature of the wounds that killed him. Without Lewis's body to prove otherwise, the crux of the controversy rests firmly in the court of public opinion.

Yet other questions remain: What happened to Lewis's dog, Seaman? If he was with Lewis that night, as the historical record suggests, why didn't he issue a warning bark?[35] Who took the money from Lewis's trunks? Why did Neelly take all of Lewis's weapons for himself? How can suicide supporters seemingly dismiss the inconsistencies in Priscilla Grinder's accounts as memory loss or hysteria? How can one explain how Lewis could have endured two wounds in vital parts of his body and still have wandered around the yard and the trace without leaving a bloody trail? What about the account of the post rider Robert O. Smith, who says he found Lewis's body near the trace and away from the buildings? If Lewis was coherent enough to ask the servants for water or to plead to be dispatched, why didn't he simply reload and finish the job? Did Lewis tell the servants someone had shot him? Perhaps his wounds were accidental? Why, if he had no intentions to do so, would Lewis write Amos Stoddard only a few weeks before his death that he intended to return to St. Louis? Why would he forward money to Washington if he did not intend to collect it? Why would Russell loan Lewis more than four months of pay and a horse and tack if he thought Lewis was mentally deranged and would not repay him? Where was Robert Grinder that night? Why didn't Jefferson launch an investigation or inquiry? Why didn't Lewis receive a proper Masonic burial?[36] Where are the notes of the 3–2 decision reached by the first coroner's inquest and the alleged trial proceedings against Robert Grinder following the incident? What are the comparative value and credibility of the contemporary textual

*The Natchez Trace. Courtesy Natchez Trace Parkway, National Park Service.*

evidence and the oral sources? How does one reconcile the conflicting, emotional, doubtful, incomplete, and incorrect evidence? These are but a sampling of the unanswered questions that the defense suggests raise reasonable doubt.[37]

Amazingly, with all of the evidence that has already been advanced, jurors must keep in mind that there were no eyewitnesses (who can be identified) who actually saw how the bullets entered Lewis's body. There was one earwitness, Priscilla Grinder, who says that after hearing the shots of two different pistols she peered through the chinking in the logs during a pitch-black, moonless night to see Lewis stumbling about the yard. She refused to give him water and did not go or send for help. Almost every other shred of the suicide account stems from her recollection of the events, supplemented by Pernier, who was likely present just before Lewis expired.

There are several inconsistencies in the contemporary testimony that raise doubt and suspicion. The written accounts of Pernier, Neelly, Russell, and especially Priscilla Grinder—nearly all of them possible suspects—contain inconsistencies and inaccuracies that call their testimony into question. Consider the possible motives of Lewis's body servant, John Pernier, whom Gilbert Russell identified as a possible accomplice and whom Lewis's mother, Lucy Marks, impugned as being somewhat responsible for the death of her son. To his credit, Pernier did travel to Virginia to visit Mrs. Marks and did report to Jefferson. Of course some might say he was simply trying to collect the $240 he claimed Lewis owed him. Tragically, he died within seven months, either by suicide or by murder made to appear self-induced.[38]

Russell's last account, offered two years after Lewis's death, was based upon a composite sketch of what he had read and heard; he mentioned Lewis's two alleged suicide attempts on the river but did not provide any details or methods. He did not say if Lewis sustained any wounds or explain why this gossip did not get picked up and printed by any of the local newspapers up and down the Mississippi. Nor do any of the earliest accounts say Lewis used a knife to cut himself. Therefore, why did Neelly start rumors stating such in the tabloids? In fact, Russell's 4 January 1810 correspondence to Jefferson indicated that Lewis's indisposition required that he be detained, but conceded that after about a week Lewis was "perfectly restored" and remained at the fort another week to see if Russell could travel with him to Washington, a request that James Wilkinson denied. A year later, Russell's story had changed. In his 26 November 1811 statement he related that Lewis arrived "in a state of mental derangement," yet still conceded the fact that after about a week was "completely in his senses" before the heat and his illness (possibly the effects of malaria) returned. Under such duress, Russell concluded, Lewis "destroyed himself, in the most Cool desperate and Barbarian-like manner." After discharging two pistols into his body, he got his razors out and "buisily engaged in cuting himself from head to foot." Interestingly, however, the accounts of Grinder and Pernier are void of any mention of self-inflicted knife wounds.

Journalist David Chandler argued that Lewis was caught up in a political conspiracy beyond his knowledge that involved former president Jefferson as well as the scoundrel General James Wilkinson, the highest-ranking military officer in the West and a well-paid "Spy No. 13" for Spain. Wilkinson had served under Benedict Arnold during the Revolutionary War, had undermined the leadership of Generals George Washington and Anthony Wayne in the years following, and had conspired with Aaron Burr to create a new nation by encouraging the secession of the territories west of the Appalachians. Ironically, Wilkinson had also been the governor of Upper Louisiana immediately before Lewis. Lewis had opposed Burr's traitorous plan and may have uncovered information linking Wilkinson to the intrigue. Certainly Lewis faced opposition in Missouri from Wilkinson's cronies.[39]

As historian J. Frederick Fausz noted, Wilkinson was a man "[s]carred by scandal, tainted by treason, and was already facing court-martial." He had real reasons to stop Lewis from proceeding to Washington and was himself ascending the Mississippi River with troops. This news must have given Lewis pause and may have been another reason for him to leave the river and venture overland. Moreover, Wilkinson, Lewis's political enemy, was responsible for the military promotions and positions of Captain Russell and Indian agent Neelly. Wilkinson had promoted Russell to major in May of 1809 and placed him in command of Fort Pickering only a few months before Lewis arrived. Fausz suggested that with Russell's "connections with, and possible obligations to, General Wilkinson, his observations about Lewis's alleged 'derangement' and alcohol abuse need to be treated with greater skepticism than most historians have done."[40]

On 5 November 1809 Surgeon's Mate W. C. Smith, the physician who cared for Lewis at Fort Pickering, wrote Secretary of War Eustis informing him that "Russell had arrested Lewis on 'charges frivolous in their nature,' had confined him to close quarters and caused him to fall ill." In addition, the Indian factor at Russell's post also sent correspondence to Washington complaining about Russell's inexperience and stability. As Richard Dillon wrote, suspect Russell "was no paragon of virtue."[41] Yet Russell personally offered to escort Lewis to Washington. Wilkinson denied the request and instead sent another one of his political appointees, James Neelly, several hundred miles out of his way to do the job.

How honest was Major James Neelly, U.S. Indian agent to the Chickasaws and a traveling partner of Lewis's? It was Neelly who entrusted a prisoner he was transporting to Nashville to someone else, rode all the way to Fort Pickering, waited for Russell's request to accompany Lewis to be denied, and then offered to escort Lewis to Nashville. Then he encouraged Lewis to drink and left him alone during his hour of greatest need. Russell even implicated Neelly in foul play and contended Lewis would still be alive if Neelly had performed his duty. Neelly conveniently arrived on the scene after Lewis had already passed away, and his accounts, like those of Russell, were based on hearsay and circumstantial evidence. Neelly waited a week before writing to inform Jefferson: "It is with extreme pain that I have to inform you of the death of His Excellency, Meriwether Lewis . . . who died on the morning of the 11th Instant and I am sorry to say by suicide."[42]

It was Neelly, then, whose accounts contain substantial contradictions, who provided most of the information that found its way into the newspapers describing Lewis's death. It was his reports that Jefferson, Clark, and others read and drew their conclusions from even though Neelly claims to have been absent when it happened and to have received his information secondhand from Mrs. Grinder. No wonder, some historians argue, the written contemporary evidence tends to support the suicide argument; most of it came from the same source—a person who admittedly was not present at the scene, provided himself as his own alibi, and is considered by some a primary murder suspect!

Physician E. G. Chuinard, for instance, has suggested that Neelly is a primary suspect. Chuinard presented a likely scenario wherein Neelly entered Lewis's room after midnight, rifled through Lewis's trunk, dazed Lewis with a shot that grazed his head, and then shot him through the body as he attempted to rise. Then Neelly fled the building before returning the next morning shortly after Lewis had expired. Finally, Chuinard found it improbable that after being shot once, Lewis was in a condition to shoot himself again, let alone live for several hours after blowing holes in major organs. Chuinard suggested Lewis died quickly after being shot, which raises additional suspicion about the accounts given by Grinder and Neelly.[43]

Neelly, with his letter to Jefferson and his conversations in Nashville, was likely the chief source of information for almost all of the contemporary accounts and published reports that appeared within two weeks of Lewis's death. His character, too, has been called into question: Why did he not remain with Lewis and send the servants to collect the strayed horses? Where was he during the night of the incident? Why did he bury the body so quickly? Despite the opportunity to preserve Lewis's body with alcohol and transport it to Nashville or Louisville, Neelly instead did not even provide Lewis a decent burial, burying him so shallow that hogs could dig him up and scatter the evidence. Why? What was he trying to hide? And what about Captain Russell's 31 January 1810 letter to Jefferson that implicated Neelly and Pernier as possible accomplices because they encouraged Lewis to drink without moderation in the days leading up to his alleged destruction of himself? Why did Neelly not return all of Lewis's personal effects to his family? Finally, why did he claim the governor owed him money when Lewis had a tremendous amount of money on his person and Neelly arrived at Fort Pickering with less than a month's wages at his disposal?

It is also interesting that another Wilkinson crony, Thomas Freeman, undertook the task of conveying Lewis's belongings to Thomas Jefferson at Monticello instead of to President Madison. Perhaps, as Laurie Winn Carlson noted, "Lewis was on his way to a very important meeting with President Madison," and "[i]f there was anything in those trunks that might have reflected negatively on Jefferson and his legacy, we can assume he [Jefferson] removed and destroyed the evidence." This was made possible only because Freeman delivered Lewis's trunks and journals to Jefferson before anyone else could see them.[44]

There are also inconsistencies between the different versions of Priscilla Grinder's accounts that need to be examined. Mrs. Grinder's multiple stories—to Neelly, to Alexander Wilson, and to an unnamed schoolteacher years later—contain several different bits of important information. Her first and second accounts indicated that Lewis behaved strangely the evening before he shot himself but omitted vital information included in that 1839 account wherein she said two or three strange men rode up to the inn that night and quarreled with Lewis.

And, she suggested, Lewis and Pernier apparently exchanged clothes after the men left, perhaps as a precaution to protect Lewis should they return. She also stated that Pernier was later wearing Lewis's expensive gold watch. Finally, she testified to hearing three shots that night, not two, which would involve another person besides Lewis firing a weapon. Could these adaptations to her story be attributed to hysteria? to forgetfulness? or had she forgotten which version of the story she was supposed to tell?

Her accounts raise additional questions. How, exactly, does a crack shot who can hit a mouse at fifty paces miss his own head and his heart at point-blank range? How does a man who has shot himself at least twice, including blowing off a portion of his forehead, wander about the cabin and its vicinity for hours? If Lewis was conscious enough to do the things the accounts suggest—ask for water, make alternate requests of people to heal his wounds or to blow his brains out, and supposedly cut his body from head to foot with a razor—why didn't he simply reload his weapons and have another go? Had Pernier taken charge of the gunpowder on purpose? Why did Priscilla Grinder, the inn's proprietor and a frontierswoman used to rough crowds, turn a deaf ear to Lewis's cries for help, particularly if his weapons were now empty? Was she acting as a cover for the real criminal, protecting a friend—or possibly her husband—or was she simply afraid of retribution from the real killer? Why didn't the servants hear the shots in the still of night and come to Lewis's aid? Where did Neely stay the night in order to conveniently arrive right after Lewis passed away? These key witnesses for suicide, then, all have some more explaining to do. After reading Vardis Fisher's *Suicide or Murder?* (the handbook for the murder theorists), even the venerable Donald Jackson, a supporter of the suicide theory, admitted that James Neely was probably a shady character and Priscilla Grinder was a nut.[45]

As one can imagine, the rumor mill and conspiracy theories have multiplied the list of possible suspects. In addition to the ones already mentioned were added Frederick Bates, land pirate Tom Runions, British agents, and Natchez Trace thugs involved in a random act of violence. Some have even suggested Jefferson may have been involved in a cover-up. To these possible suspects are added Priscilla Grinder's husband, Robert.[46] Charles Wilson, one of the earliest biographers of Lewis in the twentieth century, recorded that the "Statute Records of Tennessee show that on October 7, 1810, Griner [*sic*] was brought before a grand jury at Savannah to answer a charge of having murdered Meriwether Lewis, Governor-general of Louisiana. The case was dismissed for lack of evidence." Unfortunately, modern researchers have been unable to find the documents he cited.[47] Some twenty years ago Dee Brown wrote an article quoting a person from the area who quipped, "[E]verybody knows what happened[.] Robert Grinder came home that night, found Meriwether Lewis in bed with his wife, and shot him. The rest of the story she just made up."[48]

In refuting the conclusions by Jefferson and Clark that seem to suggest suicide, one can argue that both of their opinions were based on supposition, since both of them were far removed from the scene and relied upon newspapers, letters, or accounts from noneyewitnesses who arrived at the scene when Lewis was already dying or after he had passed away. Jefferson, too, was advancing in years and did not record the specifics of what Pernier reported to him some five weeks after the event. Moreover, Jefferson's epitaph for Lewis that appeared in the frontispiece of Biddle's *History of the Expedition* was written several years after the event and was much more negative than positive regarding his protégé. Jefferson attributed Lewis's supposed depression, hypochondria, and mental deficiencies to genetics. As a matter of fact, Jefferson's own sister Lucy, who married a Lewis, suffered from mental instability. Jefferson knew of the dozens of intermarriages between the Meriwether and Lewis families and most recently had learned that Lucy's two youngest sons, Lilburne and Isham Lewis, "were involved in a bloody and bizarre mystery of their own in Rocky Hill, Kentucky," where they apparently "decapitated a young slave with an ax in a drunken rage" and then "botched a suspected double suicide" to escape legal consequences.[49]

Jefferson was many hundreds of miles from Grinder's Stand, was retired at Monticello, and may have accepted suicide as a clean or easy way to handle the situation to protect his reputation or to prevent a possible scandal. Moreover, his slanderous comments about Lewis's instability, as Fausz has noted, probably "carry more weight than they deserve," especially since he neither witnessed nor investigated the event.[50] Claims that he suppressed an official investigation to protect James Wilkinson do not seem too likely; he had, after all, launched an extensive investigation when he heard of the apparent suicide of Sally Hemings's brother James in 1801. (The rumors proved to be true.) It is strange, however, that he apparently made no arrangements for a proper burial for Lewis, did not investigate the circumstances of his death, may have encouraged Clark to forget the whole thing, and made no record of what transpired in his meeting with Pernier or his discussion of the incident with William Clark.[51]

Lewis's mother, Lucy Marks, had reason to suspect foul play when her son's trunks were not returned to her with all personal effects—especially money, weapons, and other valuables Lewis was known to possess. Later still, an unsubstantiated story (which has since been disproved as impossible since Pernier was already deceased and Lewis's watch was listed in the personal effects turned over to Jefferson) stated that Meriwether's sister Jane and her husband supposedly met Pernier in Mobile, Alabama, and discovered that he was wearing the late governor's watch and carrying his gun. Upon being accused, the story goes, Pernier returned these articles to the Lewis family.[52]

After two centuries, some Lewis family descendants such as Howell Carr and Mary Newton Lewis steadfastly maintain that Lewis was murdered. Mary Lewis lamented that it was unfortunate that "there was no government inquiry of any kind into his death. Circumstances and events, some at the time of his death and others uncovered over the years, seem (at least to me) to substantiate that it was murder; however, the issue has never been irrevocably resolved."[53] Another relative, William Anderson, has been a vocal supporter of exhumation to help put the troubling matter to rest.

William Clark's optimism that Lewis would resolve matters in Washington and "return with flying Colours" does offset some of the trepidation he felt about his friend. In the same letter that Clark declared his fear that the weight of Lewis's mind had overcome him, he also expressed hope it was not so, saying, "I fear this report has too much truth, tho' hope it may have no foundation."[54] The entry on Lewis in a recent reference work alludes to this same conclusion, saying, "Family tradition holds that in his later years Clark became convinced that Lewis had not committed suicide after all, but had been murdered on the Natchez Trace."[55]

The murder theory gained additional momentum in the mid-nineteenth century when William Clark's eldest son, Meriwether Lewis Clark, sought to remove the perceived stigma attached to his namesake. Meriwether Lewis Clark wrote to a Reverend James Cressey of Maury County, Tennessee, "Have you heard of the report that Governor Lewis did not destroy his own life, but was murdered by his servant, a Frenchman, who stole his money and horses and returned to Natchez and was never afterwards heard of? This is an important matter in connection with the erection of a monument to his memory, as it clearly removes from my mind, at least, the only stigma upon the fair name I have the honor to bear."[56] It must be remembered that Jefferson had a long talk with William Clark about Lewis's death after Clark arrived in the East. It may be that Jefferson told Clark not to pursue the issue any further and counseled him to focus on the task of getting the journals published. This may be a clue as to why some in the Clark family questioned how Lewis died and were willing to voice those concerns shortly after their father's death in 1838.[57]

Note that Clark's son's neutral letter only presented a question, "Have you heard of the report?" and does not give proper support either way. The letter did arrive, however, about the same time the legislature of Tennessee approved spending five hundred dollars to build a fitting monument to Lewis's memory—a white granite shaft, broken at the top to indicate that Lewis died prematurely, with an inscription noting that Lewis's remains were buried at the spot. Moreover, the Meriwether Lewis Monument Committee also noted that while "the impression has long prevailed that under the influence of disease of body and mind . . . Governor Lewis perished by his own hands," it seemed "more probable that he died by the hands of an assassin."[58] No additional evidence was provided, other than the tradition that the coroner's jury found no powder burns on Lewis's body or clothes and concluded that Lewis had been shot from behind. Another tradition said Lewis had been shot from behind and left for dead in a ditch before a mail rider passing over the trace discovered the body. This news, along with other local traditions and whatever evidence was presented them, convinced the majority of the committee members that Lewis was murdered.

The strong local tradition that foul play was involved was partially substantiated by another witness who had also come forth, a woman named Polly Spencer. Spencer claimed to have been a hired girl washing the dishes the night Lewis came to Grinder's Stand. That night she heard three shots, not two. Moreover, she said that Mr. Grinder, whose wife had reported his absence in two of her accounts, actually was there and fled the scene. Accordingly, Mr. Grinder apparently was arrested and stood trial for the murder but was acquitted because of a lack of evidence.[59] These findings by Tennessee lawyer James D. Park came from Christina Anthony, a woman who had heard it from Spencer forty years previous while boarding with the Spencer family. In other words, it was hearsay evidence twice removed and more than half a century old.

Park presented another interview with a former innkeeper in Lewis County, Christina Ambrey, that appeared in the *Nashville American*. Ambrey also cast suspicion upon Robert Grinder, recalling that soon after Lewis's death, Grinder "bought a number of slaves and a farm, and seemed to have plenty of money. Before this he had always been quite poor."[60] Despite the apparent problems with the Anthony and Ambrey accounts, Park concluded that for many Tennesseans, "It has always been the firm belief of the people of this region that Governor Lewis was murdered and robbed. The oldest citizens now living remember the rumor current at the time as to the murder, and it seems that no thought of suicide ever obtained footing here."[61]

In 1893 ornithologist and historian Elliott Coues agreed, and made the first significant effort to set Lewis free from the stigma of suicide. In his *History of the Expedition under the Command of Lewis and Clark*, Coues thought Jefferson's 1813 statement on Lewis's death was flawed by both time and distance from the event. Coues apparently based his assertion that Lewis may have been murdered on the many inconsistencies found in another version of Mrs. Grinder's testimony, recorded by ornithologist Alexander Wilson and conveyed in an 1811 letter to his friend Alexander Lawson. This letter had been overlooked by historians. After comparing Priscilla Grinder's initial account and her subsequent story, Coues concluded that her testimony was unbelievable and that she was either a passive or active participant in a plot to murder Lewis. Her account, as recorded by Wilson, suggested that Lewis's muttering had kept her up all night and that after the shots were fired, she did nothing for two hours before sending the children to the barn to rouse the servants, who apparently had not been awakened by gunfire in the still of the night. For two hours Lewis supposedly implored them to give him water and help heal his wounds, then offered to pay them money to blow his brains out, to which the heartless onlookers responded by doing nothing.[62]

Once Coues had opened Pandora's box, others continued to assert that they found the murder scenario at least a possibility. A partial listing includes John Bakeless, David Chandler, E. G. Chuinard, Jonathan Daniels, Bernard DeVoto, Richard Dillon, Vardis Fisher, Ruth Colter-Frick, John Guice, James Starrs, Reuben Thwaites, Olin Wheeler, the Tennessee monument committee of 1848, and the coroner's jury of 1996. Other authors and historians also refused to accept the notion Lewis would have the disposition or inclination to kill himself. Look at his reasons to live: He had several close friends, army acquaintances, and fellow Masons; he wanted to sell his family's Virginia holdings and move his mother closer to where he could care for her; there were business opportunities in St. Louis in the fur trade and land investments; and he had successfully brought a newspaper to St. Louis and printed the laws of the territory. Even if he was not reappointed territorial governor, he likely could have received an army commission at a western post.

Ruth Colter-Frick and Grace Lewis Miller have both demonstrated that while Lewis had personal debts of about $2,750, with protested bills of about $1,958 on top of that, his land and personal assets were worth approximately $2,343. With the additional 1,600-acre land grant from Congress worth almost two dollars an acre and with his family's Virginia holdings, Lewis was land-rich and cash-poor but could have weathered the financial storm, even if he had to eventually pay all of the protested drafts.[63] Before traveling east, Lewis had named fellow Virginians Clark, Alexander Stuart, and William Carr as executors of his estate should anything happen. While stopped at New Madrid on 11 September 1809, Lewis wrote his will. He also wrote a letter to Clark that is now missing but that caused Clark to worry about his friend's mental condition. The next week, while Lewis was detained at Fort Pickering, he wrote a second will, perhaps as a portent to the precipitous collapse that lay in his immediate future. Writing a will before leaving on a long journey should not be considered a suicide note but rather a responsible act by a dutiful son naming his mother as the beneficiary of his property in the event of his unforeseen death. Lewis also wrote letters to Amos Stoddard and James Madison; these letters do not indicate his troubled mental state but actually show a sense of caution in protecting his life and property so that his valuable papers would not fall into the hands of the British.

The Natchez Trace was a dangerous place, and Lewis was well armed and prepared for possible trouble. Even Alexander Wilson, when traveling to Grinder's Stand a few years later to find out firsthand about his friend, was armed to the teeth. The Natchez Trace was definitely frequented by highwaymen who made the passage along what one author referred to as the "Devil's Backbone" a dangerous and, for some, a deadly journey.[64] A recent guidebook alluded to a Natchez Trace Parkway exhibit that reads: "This early interstate road building venture produced a snake-infested, mosquito beset, robber-haunted, Indian-pestered forest path. Lamented by the pious, cursed by the impious, it tried everyone's strength and patience."[65] Historian John Guice has added that not only was there "more than a trace of violence on that pathway to empire. The road was damned full of it."[66]

The final witnesses for the defense gave testimony in June 1996 at the National Guard armory in Hohenwald, Tennessee, about a dozen miles west of Grinder's Stand. A seven-member coroner's jury and two Tennessee district attorneys general heard the testimony of fourteen witnesses, including historians, pathologists, psychiatrists, firearms experts, document examiners, and other forensic scientists. After hearing two days of testimony from James Starrs, Arlen Large, John Guice, Ruth Colter-Frick, George Stephens, Thomas Streed, Jerry Thomas Francisco, Gerald Richards, Martin Fackler, Lucian Haag, Duayne Dillon, Reimert Ravenholt, and William Bass, the coroner's jury unanimously recommended that an on-site exhumation of Lewis's body was necessary to provide closure in this matter.[67]

Richard Dillon, author of the first full biography of Lewis, believed Lewis was murdered, likely through political intrigue, robbery, or foul play. "If there is such a person as the anti-suicide type, it was Meriwether Lewis. By temperament, he was a fighter, not a quitter."[68] The last paragraph of Dillon's book will serve as the defense's closing statement: "In a democracy such as ours—to which Meriwether Lewis was so strongly dedicated—it is held in the courts of justice that a man is presumed innocent of crime until proven guilty. Meriwether Lewis has not been proven guilty of self-destruction at Grinder's Stand in the early hours of October 11, 1809. Therefore, let him be found NOT GUILTY of the charge—the crime of suicide."[69]

Lewis's actions during the final weeks of his life indicate he was interested in living and had his wits about him. He still had concern for his health, his possessions, and his future. He had an interest in settling his accounts, clearing his name, and returning to St. Louis. No doubt Lewis suffered from malaria and perhaps even from his own futile attempts to self-treat it. Yet no previous suicide attempts can be substantiated, using multiple weapons in suicide is extremely rare, and he left no suicide note. After showing numerous plausible motives, from political conspiracies and assassination to random acts of violence and robbery; after producing a long list of probable suspects (with Neelly and the Grinders at the top); and after demonstrating that all of the contemporary evidence seemingly supporting suicide fails to hold up under scrutiny and is based on secondhand accounts and hearsay evidence emanating from some of the primary suspects, the defense rests.

As the trial concludes, one must remember who has the greater burden of proof. Since the suicide position in so widely held, the prosecutors are obligated to prove beyond a reasonable doubt that Lewis committed suicide. This creates an inequality in this particular case because the defense has only to raise doubts, which they can readily do, even though many may see their evidence and arguments as rather weak.[70] While almost everyone concedes that the written record (if taken at face value) supports the suicide theory, primary support or direct evidence is lacking and there seem to be enough inconsistencies, contractions, and unexplained phenomena to raise a reasonable doubt that Lewis took his own life. Yet, despite the motives, suspects, and rumors, not one murder theorist can definitively prove murder. Moreover, murder theories can only do damage to the suicide theory one at a time. They do not accumulate. In fact, until one strong murder theory is presented, the contradictory theories do as much damage to each other as they do to the suicide theory. No evidence of Jefferson's or Wilkinson's involvement in a conspiracy has been elevated beyond rumor or suspicion. Lewis's close friends—Clark, Jefferson, Wilson, and others— were convinced it was a suicide. It seems too easy, however, to simply say Priscilla Grinder, James Neelly, Gilbert Russell, and everyone else lied about the events of that fateful night.

In other words, there is a good deal of evidence for suicide and not much for murder. And without a body (which may or may not even exist in a condition to recover), murder theory proponents can only raise doubts by presenting a long list of suspicions, motives, and probable suspects and dispute or try to disprove the documentary evidence supporting suicide.

Phelps's conclusion in 1956 that "[i]n the absence of direct and pertinent contemporary evidence to the contrary, of which not a scintilla exists, the verdict of suicide must stand," however, cannot be definitive.[71] The American justice system is based upon the presumption of innocence until proven otherwise. Unfortunately, what has too often occurred, as E. G. Chuinard once noted, is that the so-called evidence presented is actually opinion and supposition, all too often leaving "historians quibbling over poor testimony."[72] Nels Sanddal, president and CEO of the Critical Illness and Trauma Foundation in Bozeman, Montana, has recently concluded that "as suicidologists, we somehow feel cheated if we cannot sway the determination of death to reflect our area of academic and personal curiosity. In some cases there simply isn't enough evidence. This is particularly true when the evidence is 200 years old, clouded by interpretation, and fictionalized to some unknown degree." He continued, "There are many trained historians, as well as Lewis and Clark scholars, who have pondered the manner of Lewis' death for decades. There simply is no consensus. There is no preponderance of proof to conclude that the death was either suicide, or conversely, murder. The death is, indeed, equivocal."[73]

James Holmberg and John Guice have ably addressed here the issues surrounding this important historical controversy that will likely continue to gain supporters on both sides. When numerous well-trained scholars can reach absolutely opposite opinions after consulting the same oral and written evidence, readers may do well to reconsider the factors that helped to determine their opinions and not be too hasty at reaching their own conclusions. Perhaps the National Park Services's brochure on the Natchez Trace Parkway is as close to the middle ground as anyone can come: Meriwether Lewis "died of gunshot wounds . . . under mysterious circumstances."[74]

During the Corps of Discovery's return journey from the Pacific through the summer of 1806, Lewis wanted to establish the exact location of the headwaters of the Marias River. While Clark exited Traveler's Rest to explore the Yellowstone River, Lewis and nine men crossed over Lewis and Clark Pass. Lewis left six of them to travel down the Missouri and pick up the supplies left at the portage caches made at the Great Falls. Meanwhile, he, George Drouillard, and Joseph and Reubin Field headed north to determine the true course of the Marias River. To his chagrin, Lewis discovered the Marias did not reach the 50th parallel. He stopped that night to rest at a place he named to express his mood, Camp Disappointment. After a deadly confrontation with Blackfeet on a tributary of the Marias a few days later, Lewis's party rode hard to be reunited with some of their men coming down the Missouri near the confluence of those two rivers that had posed such a mystery the previous year. Twice Lewis had been willing to search for additional, irrefutable information regarding the Marias River. First, he had redoubled his efforts to find those five glorious waterfalls that signaled to the Corps of Discovery that they had made the right choice of the true Missouri on the outbound trip. And second, he approached the Marias from another direction during the return journey. Anyone faced with understanding Lewis's death would be well served to follow his example. Like the members of the Lewis and Clark Expedition, they can take the first step by accepting the notion that either scenario is possible.

The jurors have heard the arguments addressing the uncertainty and historical controversy surrounding Meriwether Lewis's death. Their deliberation should take into consideration the comparative value of contemporary textual evidence that indicates one thing versus oral sources collected postmortem that indicate another. There is an absence of incontrovertible eyewitness proof. In addition, they should remember that most of the evidence is based on emotional responses, hearsay accounts, and information that is sometimes doubtful and occasionally incomplete or incorrect. Moreover, there are no surviving physical objects that can prove conclusively one way or the other. Without the additional physical evidence an exhumation of Lewis's body might provide, historians, scientists, physicians, and others will continue wondering, theorizing, and, undoubtedly, arguing whether his death was accidental or occurred by homicide or by suicide. As a juror you have heard both sides of the case. Deliberate carefully. The solution to one of American history's most interesting mysteries hangs on your verdict.

## Notes

1. Moulton, *Journals*, 4:248.
2. Ibid., 4:265–66.
3. Ibid., 4:271.
4. Ibid., 4:286.
5. Betts, *In Search of York*.
6. Missouri Fur Company clerk John C. Luttig recorded an entry on Sunday, 20 December 1812, that "this Evening the Wife of Charbonneau a Snake Squaw, died of a putrid fever she was a good and the best Women in the fort, aged abt 25 years she left a fine infant girl." Drumm, *Journal*, 106. William Clark cited Sacagawea as dead in his 1825–1828 list. Jackson, *Letters*, 2:638. See also Morris, *Fate of the Corps*.
7. Ella Clark and Edmonds, *Sacagawea*.
8. Thompson, "Meriwether Lewis and His Son," 24–37.
9. Dee Brown, "Mysteries of American History," 50, 52.
10. I thank William Swagerty for pointing out these and other examples of exhumations of historical figures that have yielded conclusive results through forensic science. Personal communication, 21 March 2005.
11. Robert White, "Report," 4:386.
12. *Coroner's Inquest.*

13. Starrs, "Death of a Hero," 1–6; Starrs, *Meriwether Lewis.*

14. "Senator Requests Exhumation of Meriwether Lewis," *Perspectives* (April 2002): 23.

15. Janoff, "Artist Opposes Digging Up Lewis Grave," 29–30. Janoff referenced Fisher, *Suicide or Murder?* 191–92.

16. Sassaman, "Meriwether Lewis Murder Mystery," 46.

17. Telephone conversation between Laurie Winn Carlson and Richard Williams, 11 January 2002, quoted in Carlson, *Seduced by the West,* 186, 213n45.

18. Jackson, *Letters,* 2:592.

19. Phelps, "Tragic Death," 305–18.

20. Jackson, *Letters,* 2:575, 726–27.

21. Kushner, "Suicide," 471.

22. Cutright, "Rest, Rest, Perturbed Spirit," 15–16.

23. Westefeld and Less, "Meriwether Lewis," 220, 227.

24. Moulton, *Journals,* 2:512.

25. Ambrose, *Undaunted Courage,* 461–74. Ambrose states that his first wife was "a manic-depressive who died by her own hand at the age of 28," making Lewis's possible suicide a particularly personal and poignant topic for him. Ambrose, "Reliving the Adventures."

26. Jenkinson, *Character of Meriwether Lewis,* 96–116.

27. Marian White, "Great Explorer's Final Hours," 49–50.

28. Danisi, "Ague," 10–15. Danisi is presently completing a biography of Lewis that may elucidate Lewis's supposed accidental suicide.

29. Ravenholt, "Self Destruction," 3–6; Ravenholt, "Trail's End," 1–6; Ravenholt, "Triumph Then Despair," 366–79. Some have argued that third-stage syphilis could successfully be treated by infecting the patient with malaria, whereby the resulting fevers would destroy the syphilis spirochete bacteria.

30. Nicandri, "Columbia Country," 8, 7–33 passim.

31. Holmberg, *Dear Brother,* 216–18.

32. Jones, *William Clark,* 181.

33. Foley, *Wilderness Journey,* 182.

34. Phelps, "Tragic Death," 318.

35. James Holmberg quotes an inscription made of a dog collar that read, "The greatest traveller of my species. My name is SEAMAN, the dog of captain Meriwether Lewis, whom I accompanied to the Pacifick ocean through the interior of the continent of North America." The inscription was recorded by Timothy Alden in his *A Collection of American Epitaphs and Inscriptions with Occasional Notes,* published in 1814. The entry also contained a note that said, "The foregoing was copied from the collar in the Alexandria Museum, which the late gov. Lewis's dog wore after his return from the western coast of America. The fidelity and attachment of this animal were remarkable. After the melancholy exit of gov. Lewis, his dog would not depart for a moment from his

lifeless remains, and when they were deposited in the earth no gentle means could draw him from the spot of interment. He refused to take every kind of food, which was offered him, and actually pined away and died with grief upon his master's grave!" Holmberg, "Seaman's Fate," 8.

36. Very few scholars have addressed the possible connections between Freemasonry and Lewis's death. Quite a few acquaintances of Lewis's belonged to the fraternity, including some possibly connected with his demise, such as Frederick Bates, Aaron Burr, James Wilkinson, and, believe it or not, Robert Grinder. It is likely, though it has never been verified, that his mentor Thomas Jefferson himself was a Mason, being affiliated with the *Neuf Soeurs* Lodge in Paris. It is known with certainty that Jefferson's nephews Peter and Samuel Carr were members of the Virginia brotherhood.

Lewis had received his Masonic degrees in Virginia in 1797, being initiated into the Door to Virtue Lodge No. 44 of Albemarle County and affiliated with the Widow's Son Lodge No. 60 in Charlottesville. Following his appointment as governor of Louisiana Territory, Lewis applied for a dispensation to the Grand Lodge of Pennsylvania for formation of a new St. Louis Lodge No. 111. When the new lodge was chartered on 8 November 1808, Meriwether Lewis was named its first Master of the Lodge. He served his term as master and shortly thereafter left for Washington, D.C. It was during this journey that he died on the Natchez Trace. On 18 September 1809, shortly after Lewis left St. Louis, William Clark earned his Master Mason's degree.

Freemasonry is full of allegory and symbolic meanings. Lewis had passed through the first degree, the Fellow Craft's degree, and the Master Mason's degree. These three degrees symbolize, among other things, the passage from youth to manhood and thence the sufferings and trials that culminate in death. Lewis would have been thoroughly familiar with the legend of Hiram Abif, the master architect of Solomon's temple. Even if legend, Abif's life has eerie parallels with Lewis's. Both were sons of widowed mothers. King Solomon trusted Abif with erecting a temple. President Jefferson trusted Lewis with building the American republic in upper Louisiana. Abif is said to have been killed when he refused to reveal Masonic secrets to three men involved in a conspiracy against him. Lewis may have been killed as part of a plot to protect the reputations of persons connected to the Burr conspiracy who felt threatened by information Lewis must have learned while serving as Wilkinson's successor. One of Priscilla Grinder's accounts of Lewis's death mentions three strangers who rode up to the inn that fateful night and had a passionate discussion with him before they left, opening the possibility that they, or others, returned and killed him. After his death, Abif was hastily buried in a shallow grave before his friends exhumed his body and properly reinterred it near the temple, marking the spot with a broken column to symbolize his untimely death. Lewis's body was hastily buried in a shallow grave. The three executors of his will, William Clark, Alexander Stuart, and William Carr, were

Lewis's Masonic brethren and most intimate friends, and it is curious that they, or someone else, did not recover his body and insist he be given the burial rites to which all Master Masons are entitled. Like Abif's monument, a broken pillar marked the spot of Lewis's tragic death. Finally, Eldon Chuinard noted that a member of the Grand Lodge in Helena, Montana, has claimed that his Masonic apron was in Lewis's pocket at the time of his death and that "the mysterious stains" on the apron were indeed human blood, though additional tests would have to be done to determine whether they are Lewis's blood.

In regard to Meriwether Lewis's connections to Freemasonry, see Baumler, "Masonic Apron," 54–59; Case, *Fifty . . . Military Freemasons*, 27–28; Chandler, *Jefferson Conspiracies*, 347n3; Chuinard, "Masonic Apron," 16–17; Denslow, *Territorial Masonry*, 170–95; and Adriene Price Green, Grand Lodge of Missouri, personal communication, 25 August 2005.

37. See, for instance, Chuinard, "How Did Meriwether Lewis Die?" parts 1–3; Morris, *Fate of the Corps*, 203–209.

38. Chalkley, "Man Dimly Lit," 22–26; Jackson, "On the Death."

39. Chandler, *Jefferson Conspiracies*.

40. Fausz and Gavin, "Death of Meriwether Lewis," 69–70.

41. Smith and Eustis correspondence, quoted in Dillon, *Meriwether Lewis* (1965), 347.

42. Jackson, *Letters*, 2:467.

43. Chuinard, "How Did Meriwether Lewis Die?" part 2:6–8.

44. Carlson, *Seduced by the West*, 180; Jackson, *Letters*, 2:470–72.

45. Fisher, *Suicide or Murder?* 281.

46. Two Robert Grinders appear in the 1820 census in Tennessee—one in Hickman County and one in Wayne County. See *1820 United States Federal Census*, M33 Roll 122, pp. 173, 334.

47. Charles Wilson, *Meriwether Lewis*, 281. Wilson gave the tavern owner's name as John, not Robert, and the citation he provided, which cannot be verified, read, "*Statutes*, Commonwealth of Tennessee, vol. 123, pp. 1174–78."

48. Dee Brown, "Intrigue," 88.

49. Fausz and Gavin, "Death of Meriwether Lewis," 75. See also Merrill, *Jefferson's Nephews*.

50. Fausz and Gavin, "Death of Meriwether Lewis," 74.

51. Chandler, *Jefferson Conspiracies*. Several mystery novels have also presented some creative interpretations of Lewis's death. See Hays, *Meriwether Lewis Mystery,* and Shuman, *Meriwether Murder.*

52. Kennerly and Russell, *Persimmon Hill,* 26. Note that this source contains numerous errors in addition to much credible material.

53. Mary Lewis, "Meriwether Lewis," 20.

54. Holmberg, *Dear Brother,* 216–18.

55. Tubbs, *Lewis and Clark Companion,* 195.

56. Clark Voorhis Collection, cited in Charles Wilson, *Meriwether Lewis*, 282–83.

57. Kennerly and Russell, *Persimmon Hill*.

58. Robert White, "Report," 4:385–87.

59. Fisher, *Suicide or Murder?* 214–15.

60. Quoted in Charles Wilson, *Meriwether Lewis*, 282. In 1894 Verne Pease wrote a disparaging account of the Grinder family's supposed involvement in all kinds of mischief and foul play on the trace. Pease, "Death of Captain Merriwether [*sic*] Lewis," 17–24.

61. Park, "Meriwether Lewis," quoted in Coues, *History*, 1:liii

62. Coues, *History*, 1:xliii–lxii; Alexander Wilson, "Particulars," 34–47.

63. Colter-Frick, "Meriwether Lewis's Personal Finances," 20. See also Grace Lewis Miller Papers.

64. Daniels, *Devil's Backbone*. For an alternate viewpoint, see Davis, *Way through the Wilderness*.

65. Finley, *Traveling the Natchez Trace*, xviii.

66. Guice, "Trace of Violence?" 141.

67. *Coroner's Inquest*. See also Starrs, *Meriwether Lewis*, and Zickler, "Lewis and Clark Post-Mortem."

68. Dillon, *Meriwether Lewis* (1965), 334.

69. Ibid., 349–50.

70. I thank Elliott West for pointing out the inequalities in the burden of proof and acknowledge the fact that it is easier to find holes in the suicide argument than to advance a convincing thesis for murder.

71. Phelps, "Tragic Death," 318.

72. Chuinard, "How Did Meriwether Lewis Die?" part 3:8.

73. Sanddal, "Mystery of Death," 231.

74. National Park Service, *Natchez Trace Parkway Official Map and Guide*, 1999.

# Documents

# 1. Journal entry of Meriwether Lewis, 18 August 1805.

*Suicide proponents cite this thirty-first birthday entry as evidence of depression, while others view it as an eloquent statement of ideals and plans for the future.*

The sperit of the men were now much elated at the
prospect of geting horses. —

    Courses and distances traveled by Capt. Clark
        August 17th 1805.

S 30° W. 4. to a high knob or hill in the forks of
        Jefferson's River, the same being 10 M. by
        water. the river making a considerable bend
        to the Star. the forks of this river is the
        most distant point to which the waters of
        the Missouri are navigable. of course we

Miles  4  laid up our canoes at this place and commenc
        our voyage by land. —

Sunday August 18th 1805.

    This morning while Capt Clark was busily en-
gaged in preparing for his rout, I exposed some articles to barter with the Indians for horses as I wished a
few at this moment to releive the men who were going
with Capt Clark from the labour of carrying their baggage, and also one to keep here in order to pack the
meat to camp which the hunters might kill. I soon
obtained three very good horses. for which I gave an
uniform coat, a pair of legins, a few handkerchiefs,
three knives and some other small articles the whole
of which did not cost more than about 20 $ in the
U'States. the Indians seemed quite as well pleased with
their bargin as I was. the men also purchased one for
an old checked shirt a pair of old legins and a knife.
Two of those I purchased Capt. C. took on with him.
at 10 A.M. Capt. Clark departed with his detatchment
and all the Indians except 2 men and 2 women
who remained with us. Two of the inferior chiefs were
a little displeased at not having received a present
equivolent to that given the first Chief. to releive this

difficulty Capt. Clark bestowed a couple of his old coats for them and I promised that if they were active in asist=ing me over the mountains with horses that I would give them an additional present; this seemed perfectly to satisfy them and they all set out in a good humour. Capt Clark encamped this evening near the narrow pass between the hills on Jefferson's River in the Shoshone Coves. his hunters killed one deer which the party with the aid of the Indians readily consumed in the course of the evening. — after there departure this morning I had all the stores and baggage of every discription opened and aired. and began the operation of form= ing the packages in proper parsels for the purpose of transporting them on horseback. the rain in the evening compelled me to desist from my operations. I had the raw hides put in the water in order to cut them in thrangs proper for lashing the pack= ages and forming the necesary gear for pack hors= =es, a business which I fortunately had not to learn on this occasion. Drewyer killed one deer this evening. a beaver was also caught by one of the party. I had the net arranged and set this evening to catch some trout which we could see in great abundance at the bot= =tom of the river. This day I completed my thirty first year, and conceived that I had in all human proba= =bility now existed about half the period which I am to remain in this sublunary world. I reflected that I had as yet done but little, very little indeed, to further the hapiness of the human race, or to advance the information of the succeeding generation. I viewed with regret the many hours I have spent in indolence, and now soarly feel the want of that information which these hours would have given me had they been judiciously expended. but since they are past

and cannot be recalled, I dash from me the gloomy thought 130
and resolved in future, to redouble my exertions and
at least indeavour to promote those two primary
objects of human existence, by giving them the aid
of that portion of talents which nature and fortune
have bestoed on me; or in future, to live for mankind,
as I have heretofore lived for myself. ——

---

Monday August 19th 1805.

This morning I arose at dylight and sent out three
hunters. some of the men who were much in want of
legings and mockersons I suffered to dress some skins. the
others I employed in repacking the baggage, making pack
saddles &c. we took up the net this morning but caught
no fish. one beaver was caught in a trap. the frost
which perfectly, whitened the grass this morning has
a singular appearance to me at this season. this
evening I made a few of the men construct a sain
of willow brush which we hawled and caught a large
number of fine trout and a kind of mullet about 16 Inch-
-es long which I had not seen before. the scales are small,
the nose is long and obtusely pointed and exceeds the under
jaw. the mouth is not large but opens with folds at
the sides, the colour of it's back and sides is of a bluish
brown and belley white; it has the faggot bones from
which I have supposed it to be of the mullet kind. the
tonge and pallate are smooth and it has no teeth. it
is by no means as good as the trout. the trout are
the same which I first met with at the falls of the
Missouri, they are larger than the speckled trout
of our mountains and equally as well flavored. ——
The hunters returned this evening with two deer.
from what has already been said of the Shoshones
it will be readily perceived that they live in a mode

## 2. Meriwether Lewis to President James Madison, Chickasaw Bluffs, 16 September 1809.

*There is disagreement over whether this letter is credible evidence of Lewis's mental deterioration.*

when fully explained, or rather the ge-
-neral view of the circumstances under
which they were made I flatter myself
~~that~~ they will receive both ~~approbation~~ and
sanction.—

Provided my health permits no time
shall be lost in reaching Washington,
My anxiety to pursue and to fullfill the
duties incident to the internal arrangements
incedent to the government of Louisiana
has prevented my writing you more frequently.
~~Mr. Bates left in day~~— I inclose I
herewith transmit you a copy of the
laws of the territory of Louisiana.—
I have the honour to be with the most
sincere esteem Your Obt. ~~and very humble~~

Oft. and very humble Servt. —

Meriwether Lewis.

James Madison Esqr.
President U States

Courtesy of the Missouri Historical Society.

## 3. Meriwether Lewis to Major Amos Stoddard, Chickasaw Bluffs, 22 September 1809 (page 1).

*Lewis requests that Stoddard send Lewis's money to Washington, D.C., and informs his friend of plans to return to St. Louis after rectifying affairs.*

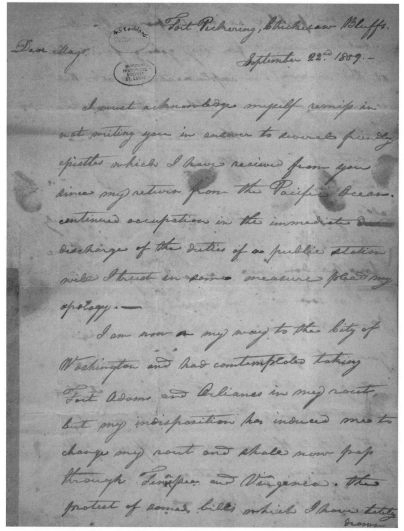

Courtesy of the Missouri Historical Society.

## 4. James Neelly to Thomas Jefferson, Nashville, Tennessee, 18 October 1809.

Nashville, Tennessee, 18th Octr. 1809

Sir,

It is with extreme pain that I have to inform you of the death of His Excellency, Meriwether Lewis, Governor of upper Louisiana who died on the morning of the 11th Instant and I am sorry to say by suicide.

I arrived at the Chickasaw Bluffs on or about the 18th of September, where I found the Governor (who had reached there two days before me from St. Louis) in very bad health. It appears that his first intention was to go around by water to the City of washington; but his thinking a war with England probable, & that his valuable papers might be in dainger of falling into the hands of the British, he was thereby induced to Change his route, and to come through the Chickasaw nation by land; I furnished him with a horse to pack his trunks &c. on, and a man to attend to them; having recovered his health in some degree at the Chickasaw Bluffs, we set out together and on our arrival at the Chickasaw nation I discovered that he appeared at times deranged in mind, we rested there two days & came on. one days Journey after crossing Tennessee River & where we encamped we lost two of our horses, I remained behind to hunt them & the Governor proceeded on, with a promise to wait for me at the first houses he came to that was inhabited by white people; he reached the house of a Mr. Grinder about sun set. the man of the house being from home, and no person there but a woman who discovering the governor to be deranged gave him up the house & slept herself in one near it. his servant and mine slept in the stable loft some distance from the other houses, the woman reports that about three o'clock she heard two pistols fire off in the Governors Room. the servants being awakined by her, came in but too late to save him. he had shot himself in the head with one pistol & a little below the Breast with the other. when his servant came in he says; I have done the business my good servant give me some water. he gave him water, he survived but a short time, I came up some time after, & had him as decently Buried as I could in that place. if there is any thing wished by his friends to be done to his grave I will attend to their Instructions.

I have got in my possession his two trunks of papers (amongst which is said to be his travels to the pacific ocean) and probably some Vouchers for expenditures of Public money for a Bill which he said had been

protested by the Secy. Of War, and of which act to his death, he repeatedly complained. I have also in my care his Rifle, Silver watch, Brace of
Pistols, dirk & tomahawk: one of the Governors horses was lost in the
wilderness which I will endeavour to regain, the other I have sent on by
his servant who expressed a desire to go to the governors mothers & to
montic[e]llo: I have furnished him with fifteen Dollars to Defray his
expences to charlottsville; Some days previous to the Governors death
he requested of me in case any accident happened to him, to send his
trunks with the papers therein to the President, but I think it very probable he meant to you. I wish to be informed what arrangements may be
considered best in sending on his trunks &c. I have the honor to be with
Great respect Yr. Ob. Sert.

James Neelly<br>
U. S. agent to the Chickasaw nation

the Governor left two of his trunks at the Chickasaw Bluffs in the
care of Capt. Gilbert C. Russell, commanding officer, & was to write to
him from Nashville what to do with them.

Source: Thomas Jefferson Papers, Library of Congress; Donald D. Jackson,
ed., *Letters of the Lewis and Clark Expedition with Related Documents, 1783–1834*,
2d edition, 2:467–48.

## 5. William Clark to Jonathan Clark, Mr. Shannons, Shelby County, Kentucky, 28 October 1809.

*In this letter Clark expresses his dismay regarding the reported suicide of Lewis and his belief that his partner in discovery might have taken his own life.*

particular friend of his and on his way to the City of
Washington? and set out from the Bluff with a
view to prop. this, the Work sent out, which is
by Nashville. ... O. ... the usage of his friend
has over come him, what will be the consequence
...
what will become of my papers? I must write to
Genl Robinson or some friend about Rochester to
engrave about him, and collect and send me
his papers, if he had any with them - I am gratified
about this refusal.

## 6. William Clark to Jonathan Clark, Bean Station, Tennessee, 8 November 1809.

*Clark's letter relates his hope to learn more about Lewis's death and confesses that the death was a "turble Stroke to me."*

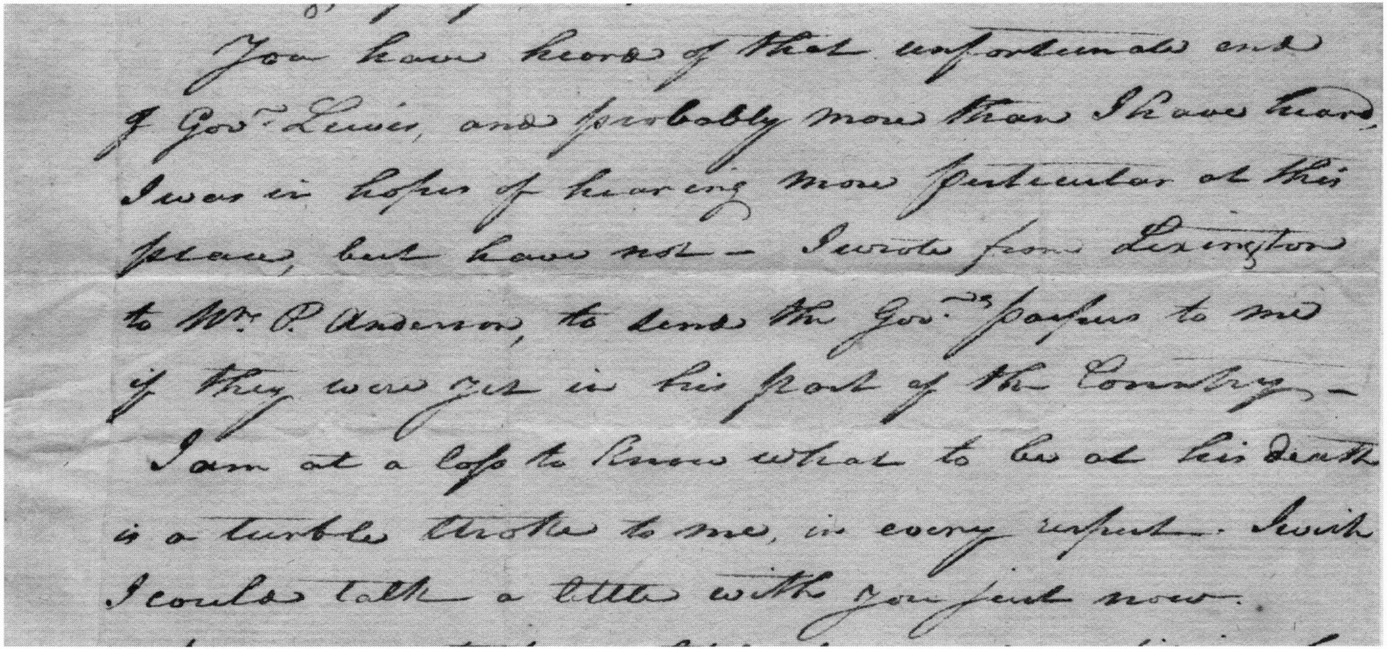

## 7. William Clark to Jonathan Clark, Colonel Hancocks, 26 November 1809.

*As he learns more concerning Lewis's death, Clark reports it to his brother Jonathan. In this letter he reveals important news he has received from Gilbert Russell and John Pernier.*

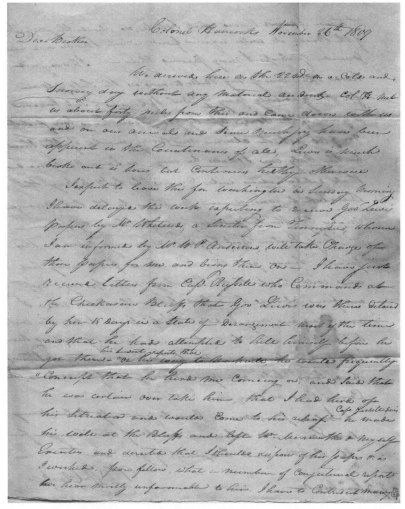

Courtesy of the Filson Historical Society.

## 8. Alexander Wilson to Alexander Lawson, Natchez, Mississippi Territory, 28 May 1811.

*Wilson devotes part of his letter to an account of his visit to Grinder's Stand and Lewis's death as recounted by Priscilla Grinder.*

Next morning (Sunday) I rode six miles to a man's of the name of Grinder, where our poor friend Lewis perished. In the same room where he expired, I took down from Mrs. Grinder the particulars of that melancholy event, which affected me extremely. This house or cabin is seventy-two miles from Nashville, and is the last white man's as you enter the Indian country. Governor Lewis, she said, came there about sunset, alone, and inquired if he could stay for the night; and, alighting, brought his saddle into the house. He was dressed in a loose gown, white, striped with blue. On being asked if he came alone, he replied that there were two servants behind, who would soon be up. He called for some spirits, and drank a very little. When the servants arrived, one of whom was a negro, he inquired for his powder, saying he was sure he had some powder in a cannister. The servant gave no distinct reply, and Lewis, in the mean while, walked backwards and forwards before the door, talking to himself. Sometimes, she said, he would seem as if he were walking up to her; and would suddenly wheel round, and walk back as fast as he could. Supper being ready he sat down, but had not eat but a few mouthfuls, when he started up, speaking to himself in a violent manner. At these times, she says, she observed his face to flush as if it had come on him in a fit. He lighted his pipe, and drawing a chair to the door sat down, saying to Mrs. Grinder, in a kind tone of voice, "Madam this is a very pleasant evening." He smoked for some time, but quitted his seat and traversed the yard as before. He again sat down to his pipe, seemed again composed, and casting his eyes wishfully towards the west, observed what a sweet evening it was. Mrs. Grinder was preparing a bed for him; but he said he would sleep on the floor, and desired the servant to bring the bear skins and buffaloe robe, which were immediately spread out for him; and it being now dusk the woman went off to the kitchen, and the two men to the barn, which stands about two hundred yards off. The kitchen is only a few paces from the room where Lewis was, and the woman being considerably alarmed by the behaviour of her guest could not sleep, but listened to his walking backwards and forwards, she thinks, for several hours, and talking aloud, as she said, "like a lawyer." She then heard the report of a pistol, and something fall heavily on the floor, and the words *"O Lord!"* Immediately afterwards she heard another pistol, and in a few minutes she heard him at her door calling out *"O madam! give me some water, and heal my wounds."* The logs being open, and unplastered, she saw him stagger back and fall against a stump that stands between the kitchen and the room. He crawled for some distance, raised himself by the side of a tree, where he sat about a minute. He once more got to the room; afterwards he came to the kitchen door, but did not speak; she then heard him scraping the bucket with a gourd for water; but it appears that this cooling element was denied the dying man! As soon as day broke and not before, the terror of the woman having permitted him to remain for two hours in this most deplorable situation, she sent two of her children to the barn, her husband not being home, to bring the servants; and on going in they found him lying on the bed; he uncovered his side and showed them where the bullet had entered; a piece of the forehead was blown off, and had exposed the brains, without having bled much. He begged they would take his rifle and blow out his brains, and he would give them all the money he had in his trunk. He often said, "I am no coward; but I am *so* strong, *so hard to die."* He begg'd the servant not to be afraid of him, for that he would not hurt him. He expired in about two hours, or just as the sun rose above the trees. He lies buried close by the common path, with a few loose rails thrown over his grave. I gave Grinder money to put a post fence around it, to shelter it from the hogs, and from the wolves; and he gave me his written promise he would do it. I left this place in a very melancholy mood, which was not much allayed by the prospect of the gloomy and savage wilderness which I was just entering alone.

Source: "Particulars of the Death of Capt. Lewis," *The Port Folio* 7, no. 1 (January 1812): 36–38.

## 9. Statement of Gilbert C. Russell, 26 November 1811.

Governor Lewis left St. Louis late in August, or early in September 1809, intending to go by the route of the Mississippi and the Ocean, to the City of Washington, taking with him all the papers relative to his expedition to the pacific Ocean, for the purpose of preparing and puting them to the press, and to have some drafts paid which had been drawn by him on the Government and protested. On the morning of the 15th of September, the Boat in which he was a passenger landed him at Fort pickering in a state of mental derangement, which appeared to have been produced as much by indisposition as other causes. The Subscriber being then the Commanding Officer of the Fort on discovering his situation, and learning from the Crew that he had made two attempts to Kill himself, in one of which he had nearly succeeded, resolved at once to take possession of him and his papers, and detain them there untill he recovered, or some friend might arrive in whose hands he could depart in Safety.

In this condition he continued without any material change for about five days, during which time the most proper and efficatious means that could be devised to restore him was administered, and on the sixth or Seventh day all symptoms of derangement disappeared and he was completely in his senses and thus continued for ten or twelve days. On the 29th of the same month he left Bluffs, with the Chickasaw agent the interpreter and some of the Chiefs, intending then to proceed the usual route thro' the Indian Country, Tennessee and Virginia to his place of distination, with his papers well secured and packed on horses. By much severe depletion during his illness he had been considerably reduced and debilitated, from which he had not entirely recovered when he set off, and the weather in that Country being yet excessively hot and the exercise of traveling too Severe for him; in three or four days he was again affected with the same mental disease. He had no person with him who could manage or controul him in his propensities and he daily grew worse untill he arrived at the house of a Mr. Grinder within the Jurisdiction of Tennessee and only Seventy miles from Nashville, where in the apprehension of being destroyed by enemies which had no existence but in his wild immagination, he destroyed himself, in the most Cool desperate and Barbarian-like manner, having been left in the house intirely to himself. The night preceeding this one of his Horses and one of the Chickasaw agents with whom he was traveling Strayed off from the

Camp and in the morning could not be found.

The agent with some Indians Stayed to Search for the horses, and Governor Lewis with their two Servants and the baggage horses proceeded to Mr. Grinders where he was to halt untill the agent got up.

after he arrived there and refreshed himself with a little meal & drink he went to bed in a cabin by himself and ordered the Servants to go to the Stables and take care of the Horses, least they might loose some that night;

Some time in the night he got his pistols which he loaded, after every body had retired in a Seperate Building and discharged one against his forehead without much effect—the ball not penetrating the Skull but only making a furrow over it. He then discharged the other against his breast where the ball entered and passing downward thro' his body came out low down near his back bone. after Some time he got up and went to the house where Mrs. Grinder and her children were lying and asked for water, but her husband being absent and having heard the report of the pistols She was greatly allarmed and made him no answer. He then in returning got his razors from a port folio which happened to contain them and Seting up in his bed was found about day light, by one of the Servants, buisily engaged in cuting himself from head to foot. He again beged for water, which was given him and so soon as he drank, he lay down and died with the declaration to the Boy that he had Killed himself to deprive his enemies of the pleasure and honor of doing it. His death was greatly leamented. And that a fame so dearly earned as his Should finally be Clouded by Such an act of desperation was to his friends Still greater Cause of regret.

(Signed) Gilbert Russell

The above was received by me from Major Gilbert Russell of the [*blank*] Regiment of Infantry U. S. on Tuesday the 26th of November 1811 at Fredericktown in Maryland.

J. Williams

Source: Jonathan Williams Manuscripts, Lilly Library, Indiana University; Donald D. Jackson, ed., *Letters of the Lewis and Clark Expedition with Related Documents, 1783–1834,* 2d edition, 2:573–74.

# Varying Views of Meriwether Lewis's Death

| | Suicide Advocates | Homicide Advocates |
|---|---|---|
| 1809 | Frederick Bates, in Marshall, *Life & Papers* | Lucy Marks |
| | John Brahan, in Jefferson Papers | John Treat, in Dillon, *Meriwether Lewis* |
| | William Clark, in Holmberg, *Dear Brother* | |
| | Priscilla Grinder, James Neelly, and John Pernier, in Jackson, *Letters* | |
| 1809 | Gilbert Russell, in Jackson, *Letters* | |
| 1810 | Thomas Jefferson, in Jackson, *Letters* | |
| 1812 | Alexander Wilson, in *Port Folio* | |
| 1814 | Thomas Jefferson, in Biddle/Allen, *History* | |
| 1848 | | White, "Report of Monument Committee" |
| 1891/1903 | | Park [a.k.a. John Quill], "Lewis" |
| 1893 | | Coues, *History of the Expedition* |
| 1894 | | Pease, "Death of Captain Lewis" |
| 1901 | | Brooks, *First across the Continent* |

|      | Suicide Advocates | Homicide Advocates |
|------|-------------------|--------------------|
| 1904 | John Moore, "Death of Lewis" | Thwaites, *Original Journals* |
|      |                   | Webster, "Death of Gen. Lewis" |
|      |                   | Wheeler, *Trail of Lewis and Clark* |
| 1925 |                   | Denslow, *Territorial Masonry* |
| 1933 |                   | Kellogg, "Meriwether Lewis" |
| 1937 |                   | Gwathmey, *Twelve Virginia Counties* |
| 1947 |                   | Bakeless, *Lewis and Clark* |
| 1948 |                   | Kennerly and Russell, *Persimmon Hill* |
| 1953 |                   | DeVoto, *Journals of Lewis and Clark* |
| 1955 |                   | Case, *Fifty . . . Military Masons* |
| 1956 | Phelps, "Tragic Death" |               |
| 1962 |                   | Fisher, *Suicide or Murder?* |
|      |                   | Daniels, *Devil's Backbone* |
| 1965 |                   | Dillon, *Meriwether Lewis* |
| 1976 | Merrill, *Jefferson's Nephews* |      |
| 1978 | Jackson, *Letters of Lewis & Clark* | |
| 1981 | Kushner, "Suicide of Meriwether Lewis" | |
| 1986 | Moulton, *Journals . . . Expedition* | |
|      | Cutright, "Rest, Rest, Perturbed Spirit" | |
| 1991 |                   | Chuinard, "How Did . . . Die?" |
| 1992 | Holmberg, "I Wish You to See . . ." | |
| 1994 | Ravenholt, "Triumph Then Despair" | Chandler, *Jefferson Conspiracies* |
| 1995 |                   | Guice, "Fatal Rendezvous" |
| 1996 | Ambrose, *Undaunted Courage* | *Coroner's Inquest* |
| 1997 |                   | Starrs, *Meriwether Lewis* |
| 1999 | Jamison, *Night Falls Fast* | |
| 2000 | Jenkinson, *Character of Meriwether Lewis* | |

| 2002 | Holmberg, *Dear Brother* | *We Proceeded On* (February & May issues) |
|------|--------------------------|-------------------------------------------|
|      | Peck, *Or Perish in the Attempt* | Saindon, "Unhappy Affair" |
|      | Danisi, " 'Ague' Made Him Do It" | |
| 2004 | Jones, *William Clark* | Fausz and Gavin, "Meriwether Lewis" |
|      | Morris, *Fate of the Corps* | |
|      | Foley, *Into the Wilderness* | |
|      | Westefeld and Less, "Meriwether Lewis" | |
| 2005 | Nicandri, "Columbia Country" | Baumler, "Masonic Apron" |

# Selected Bibliography

## COMPILED BY JAY H. BUCKLEY

### Manuscripts

William Clark Memorandum Book, 1809. Breckenridge Collection, State Historical Society of Missouri, Columbia.

Duncan Cooper Papers. Tennessee State Library and Archives, Nashville.

Cooper Family Papers. Tennessee State Library and Archives, Nashville.

*Coroner's Inquest: Death of Meriwether Lewis.* Transcript of the Proceedings before the Coroner and Jury of Lewis County at Hohenwald, Tenn., 3–4 June 1996, pp. 1–364. Franklin, Tenn.: Anita F. Polk, Franklin Court Reporters, 1996.

Lyman C. Draper Manuscripts. Wisconsin Historical Society, Madison.

Eva Emery Dye Papers, Oregon Historical Society, Portland.

Vardis Fisher Papers, Donald Jackson File, Beinecke Library, Yale University, New Haven, Conn.

Hamilton, William B. "American Beginnings in the Old Southwest: The Mississippi Phase." Ph.D. dissertation, Duke University, 1938.

Thomas Jefferson Papers, Library of Congress, Washington, D. C. American Memory Online Collection. http://memory.loc.gov/ammem/.

Grace Lewis Miller Papers, Jefferson National Expansion Memorial, National Park Service, St. Louis, Mo.

Meriwether Lewis Memorial Association Papers, 1880–1931. Microfilm 1374. Number 93-001, XIV-L-2, II-D-1v. Tennessee State Library and Archives, Nashville.

Meriwether Lewis Scrapbook, 1774–1935. Microfilm 1054. TSLA, 1 reel. Tennessee State Library and Archives, Nashville.

Meriwether Lewis vertical file. Tennessee State Library and Archives, Nashville.

Old Oak Club Papers. "Suicide: The Case of Meriwether Lewis." A Paper Presented by Joseph May at the Old Oak Club 27 April 1972. V-M-1, Box 1. Tennessee State Library and Archives, Nashville.

Jonathan Williams Manuscripts. Lilly Library, Indiana University, Bloomington.

## Newspapers (with no named authors)

*Frankfort (Ky.) Argus of Western America*, 1809.
*Nashville (Tenn.) Democratic Clarion*, 20 October 1809.
*Philadelphia Saturday American*, 7 December 1844, in Draper Mss., 29CC56; essentially the same story appeared in the *New York Dispatch*, 1 February 1845, in Draper Mss., 29CC33, and was almost certainly picked up from the former, which originally got the story from the *North Arkansas*, a newspaper in Batesville, Ark.
*Russellville (Ky.) Farmer's Friend*, 27 October 1809.
*St. Louis Missouri Gazette*, 2 and 23 November 1809.
*Washington (D.C.) Niles' National Register*, 18 August 1838, 54: 394–95. The information was reprinted from the *New York Evening Star*.

## Books and Articles

Abrams, Rochonne. "The Colonial Childhood of Meriwether Lewis." *Bulletin of the Missouri Historical Society* 34 (October 1977–July 1978): 218–27.
Ambrose, Stephen E. "Reliving the Adventures of Meriwether Lewis." *We Proceeded On* 29, no. 1 (February 2003): 11–13.
———. *Undaunted Courage: Meriwether Lewis, Thomas Jefferson, and the Opening of the West*. New York: Simon & Schuster, 1996.
Bakeless, John. *Lewis and Clark: Partners in Discovery*. New York: William Morrow, 1947.
Baumler, Ellen. "The Masonic Apron of Meriwether Lewis and the Legacy of Masonry in Montana." *Montana The Magazine of Western History* 55, no. 4 (Winter 2005): 54–59.
Betts, Robert B. *In Search of York: The Slave Who Went to the Pacific with Lewis and Clark*. Rev. ed. Boulder: University Press of Colorado, 2000.
Biddle, Nicholas, and Paul Allen, eds. *History of the Expedition under the Command of Captains Lewis and Clark, to the Sources of the Missouri, Thence across the Rocky Mountains and down the River Columbia to the Pacific Ocean. Performed during the Years 1804–5–6. By Order of the Government of the United States*. 2 vols. Philadelphia: Bradford and Inskeep; New York: Abraham Inskeep, 1814.
Boyd, Julian P. "These Precious Monuments of Our History." *The American Archivist* 22 (April 1959): 147–80.
Brandt, Anthony. "The Perilous Afterlife of the Lewis and Clark Expedition." *American Heritage* 55 (June/July 2004): 50–58.
Brooks, Noah. *First across the Continent: The Story of the Exploring Expedition of Lewis and Clark in 1804–5–6*. New York: C. Scribner's Sons, 1901.

Brown, D. Alexander. "The Mysterious Death of a Hero." *American History Illustrated* 5, no. 9 (January 1971): 18–27.

Brown, Dee. "Intrigue on the Natchez Trace." *Southern Magazine* (November 1986): 43–44, 74, 88.

——. "Mysteries of American History—How Did Meriwether Lewis Die?" *American Heritage* 41 (December 1990): 52.

——. "What Really Happened to Meriwether Lewis? The Suicide Explanation Is Not Generally Believed Down on the Natchez Trail." *Columbia: The Magazine of Northwest History* 1, no. 4 (Winter 1988). This is a reprint of the *Southern Magazine* article.

Brown, Vicki. "An Unsettling Death." *New Orleans Gambit Weekly*, 20 May 2003.

Buckley, Jay H. *William Clark: Indian Agent*. Norman: University of Oklahoma Press, in press.

Carlson, Laurie W. *Seduced by the West: Jefferson's America and the Lure of the Land beyond the Mississippi*. Chicago: Ivan R. Dee, 2003.

Carter, Clarence E., ed. *The Territorial Papers of the United States*. 28 vols. Washington: Government Printing Office, 1934–1975. [Neelly to Jefferson, 18 October 1809, 14: 332–34.]

Case, James R. *Fifty Early American Military Freemasons*. Bethel, Conn.: Grand Lodge of Connecticut, 1955.

Chalkley, Mark. "A Man Dimly Lit by History: Was John Pernier, Meriwether Lewis's 'Faithful Servant,' in Fact His Murderer? The Allegation Is Doubtful." *We Proceeded On* 30, no. 4 (November 2004): 22–26.

——. "Paul Allen: 'Editor' of the Lewis & Clark Journals." *We Proceeded On* 28, no. 3 (August 2002): 8–11.

Chandler, David L. *The Jefferson Conspiracies: A President's Role in the Assassination of Meriwether Lewis*. New York: William Morrow, 1994.

Chuinard, Eldon G. "How Did Meriwether Lewis Die? It Was Murder." Parts 1–3. *We Proceeded On* 17, no. 3 (August 1991): 4–12; 17, no. 4 (November 1991): 4–10; 18, no. 1 (January 1992): 4–10.

——. "The Masonic Apron of Meriwether Lewis." *We Proceeded On* 15, no. 1 (February 1989): 16–17.

——. *Only One Man Died: The Medical Aspects of the Lewis and Clark Expedition*. Glendale, Calif.: Arthur H. Clark, 1979.

Clark, Ella, and Margot Edmonds, *Sacagawea of the Lewis and Clark Expedition*. Berkeley: University of California Press, 1979.

Clark, Thomas D., and John D. W. Guice. *The Old Southwest, 1795–1830: Frontier in Conflict*. Norman: University of Oklahoma Press, 1996.

Coates, Robert M. *The Outlaw Years: The History of the Land Pirates of the Natchez Trace*. New York: Macaulay Company, 1930.

Colter-Frick, L. Ruth. "Meriwether Lewis's Personal Finances." *We Proceeded On* 28, no. 1 (February 2002): 16–20.

Coues, Elliott, ed. *The History of the Lewis and Clark Expedition*. 3 vols. 1893. Reprint. New York: Dover Publications, 1965.

Cutright, Paul Russell. "Contributions of Philadelphia to Lewis and Clark History." *We Proceeded On, Supplementary Publication* 6, no. 2 (1982): 21–29.

——. "Rest, Rest, Perturbed Spirit." *We Proceeded On* 12, no. 1 (March 1986): 7–16.

Daniels, Jonathan. *The Devil's Backbone: The Story of the Natchez Trace*. New York: McGraw-Hill, 1962.

Danisi, Thomas C. "The 'Ague' Made Him Do It." *We Proceeded On* 28, no. 1 (February 2002): 10–15.

Davis, William C. *A Way through the Wilderness: The Natchez Trace and the Civilization of the Southern Frontier*. New York: HarperCollins, 1995.

Denslow, Ray V. *Territorial Masonry: The Story of Freemasonry and the Louisiana Purchase*. 1925. Reprint, Whitefish, Mont.: Kessinger, 1997.

DeVoto, Bernard. *The Journals of Lewis and Clark*. Boston: Houghton Mifflin, 1953.

Dillon, Richard H. *Meriwether Lewis: A Biography*. New York: Coward-McCann, 1965. Paperback reprint, with foreword by Stephen Ambrose. Santa Cruz, Calif.: Tanager Press, 1988.

——. *The Search for Meriwether Lewis: From Tillamook to Grinder's Stand*. [C. C. Williamson Memorial Lecture]. Nashville: George Peabody College for Teachers, 1967.

Drumm, Stella M., ed. *Journal of a Fur-Trading Expedition on the Upper Missouri 1812–1813*. New York: Argosy-Antiquarian, 1964.

Dye, Eva Emery. *The Conquest*. 1902. Rev. ed. New York: Wilson-Erickson, 1936.

Fausz, J. Frederick, and Michael A. Gavin. "The Death of Meriwether Lewis: An Unsolved Mystery." *Gateway Heritage* 24, nos. 2–3 (Fall 2003–Winter 2004): 66–79.

Finley, Lori. *Traveling the Natchez Trace*. Winston-Salem, N.C.: John F. Blair, 1995.

Fisher, Vardis. *Suicide or Murder?: The Strange Death of Governor Meriwether Lewis*. Denver: Alan Swallow, 1962.

Foley, William E. *Wilderness Journey: The Life of William Clark*. Columbia: University of Missouri Press, 2004.

Garrision, Dwight. "Lewis Is Not Alone." *We Proceeded On* 13, no. 4 (November 1987): 10–11.

Guice, John D. W. "A Fatal Rendezvous: The Mysterious Death of Meriwether Lewis." *Journal of Mississippi History* 57, no. 2 (1995): 121–38.

——. " 'A Fatal Rendezvous': The Mysterious Death of Meriwether Lewis." *We Proceeded On* 24, no. 2 (May 1998): 4–12.

——. "Fisher and Meriwether Lewis." In *Rediscovering Vardis Fisher: Centennial Essays*, edited by Joseph M. Flora. Moscow: University of Idaho Press, 2000.

——. "A Trace of Violence?" *Southern Quarterly* 29 (Summer 1991): 123–43.

——. "Moonlight and Meriwether Lewis." *We Proceeded On* 28, no. 1 (February 2002): 21–25.

Gwathmey, John H. *Twelve Virginia Counties: Where the Western Migration Began.* Richmond, Va.: Dietz Press, 1937.

Hays, Wilma P. *The Meriwether Lewis Mystery.* Philadelphia: Westminister Press, 1971.

Heitman, Francis B., comp. *Historical Register and Dictionary of the United States Army, from Its Organization, September 29, 1789, to March 2, 1903.* 1903. Reprint, Urbana: University of Illinois Press, 1965.

Holmberg, James J., ed. *Dear Brother: Letters of William Clark to Jonathan Clark.* New Haven: Yale University Press, 2002.

——. " 'I Wish You to See & Know All': The Recently Discovered Letters of William Clark to Jonathan Clark." *We Proceeded On* 18, no. 4 (November 1992): 4–12.

——. Review of *The Jefferson Conspiracies: A President's Role in the Assassination of Meriwether Lewis* by David Chandler, in *We Proceeded On* 21, no. 3 (August 1995): 27–29.

——. "Seaman's Fate: Lewis's Dog Probably Survived Him." *We Proceeded On* 26, no. 1 (February 2000): 7–9.

Jackson, Donald D. *Among the Sleeping Giants: Occasional Pieces on Lewis and Clark.* Urbana: University of Illinois Press, 1987.

——, ed. *Letters of the Lewis and Clark Expedition with Related Documents, 1783–1854.* 2 vols. 2d ed. Urbana: University of Illinois Press, 1978.

——. "On the Death of Meriwether Lewis's Servant." *William and Mary Quarterly* 21 (July 1964): 445–48.

Jamison, Kay Redfield. *Night Falls Fast: Understanding Suicide.* New York: Alfred A. Knopf, 1999.

Jenkinson, Clay S. *The Character of Meriwether Lewis: "Completely Metamorphosed" in the American West.* Reno, Nev.: Marmarth Institute, 2000.

Janoff, Larry. "Artist Opposes Digging Up Lewis Grave." *We Proceeded On* 22, no. 4 (November 1996): 29–30.

Jones, Landon Y. *William Clark and the Shaping of the West.* New York: Farrar Straus and Giroux, 2004.

Kellogg, Louise. "Meriwether Lewis." *Dictionary of American Biography.* New York: Charles Scribner's Sons, 1933.

Kennerly, William Clark, and Elizabeth Russell. *Persimmon Hill: A Narrative of Old St. Louis and the Far West.* Norman: University of Oklahoma Press, 1948.

Kushner, Howard I. "The Suicide of Meriwether Lewis: A Psychoanalytic Inquiry." *William and Mary Quarterly* 38 (July 1981): 464–81.

Kvernes, David, ed. *The Lewis and Clark Expedition: Then and Now.* Sioux Falls, S.Dak.: Center for Western Studies, Augustana College, 2004.

Lange, Robert E. "Meriwether Lewis Monument, Natchez Trace Parkway, near Hohenwald, Tennessee." *We Proceeded On* 17, no. 1 (March 1986): 12.

Lewis, E. C. "Meriwether Lewis's Death." *Nashville (Tenn.) American*, 25 May 1904. Letter to editor.

Lewis, Mary N. "Meriwether Lewis: Devoted Son." *We Proceeded On* 16, no. 2 (May 1990): 14–20.

Lewis, William Terrell. *Genealogy of the Lewis Family in America.* Louisville: Courier-Journal Printing Co., 1893.

Loge, Ronald V. "Meriwether Lewis and Malaria." *We Proceeded On* 28, no. 2 (May 2002): 33–35.

McAllister, John Meriwether, and Lura Boulton Tandy, eds. *Genealogies of the Lewis and Kindred Families.* Columbia, Mo.: E. W. Stephens, 1906.

Marshall, Thomas M., ed. *The Life and Papers of Frederick Bates.* 2 vols. St. Louis: Missouri Historical Society, 1926.

Merrill, Boynton, Jr. *Jefferson's Nephews: A Frontier Tragedy.* Lincoln: University of Nebraska Press, 2004.

Moore, Bob. "Corps of Discovery Gravesites." *We Proceeded On* 26, no. 2 (May 2000): 5–9.

Moore, John H. "The Death of Meriwether Lewis." *American Historical Magazine* 9 (1904): 218–30.

Moore, Kathryn. "The Lost Years of Meriwether Lewis." *Journal of the West* 42, no. 3 (2003): 58–65.

Morris, Larry E. "After the Expedition." *American History* 38, no. 1 (2003): 44–56, 58, 60.

———. *The Fate of the Corps: What Became of the Lewis and Clark Explorers after the Expedition.* New Haven, Conn.: Yale University Press, 2004.

Moulton, Gary E., ed. *The Journals of the Lewis and Clark Expedition.* 13 vols. Lincoln: University of Nebraska Press, 1983–2001.

National Park Service. *Natchez Trace Parkway Official Map and Guide*, 1999.

Nicandri, David L. "The Columbia Country and the Dissolution of Meriwether Lewis: Speculations and Interpretations." *Oregon Historical Quarterly* 106, no. 1 (Spring 2005): 7–33.

Park, James D. "Meriwether Lewis . . . ." *Nashville (Tenn.) American*, 4 January 1903. Reprint of article under pseudonym John Quill in *Nashville American*, 6 September 1891.

Pease, Verne S. "The Death of Captain Merriwether [*sic*] Lewis." *Southern Magazine* (February 1894): 17–24.

Peck, David J. *Or Perish in the Attempt: Wilderness Medicine in the Lewis & Clark Expedition.* Helena, Mont.: Farcountry Press, 2002.

Pedersen, Daniel. "Lewis's Mysterious End." *Newsweek* 128 (28 October 1996): 67.

Phelps, Dawson A. "The Tragic Death of Meriwether Lewis." *William and Mary Quarterly* 13 (July 1956): 305–18.

Pilcher, Margaret Campbell. *Historical Sketches of the Campbell, Pilcher and Kindred Families*. Nashville, Tenn.: Marshall & Bruce, 1911.

Ravenholt, Reimert T. "Did Stephen Ambrose Sanitize Meriwether Lewis's Death?" http://www.historynewsnetwork.org; (8 April 2002): 1–3.

——. "Doctor Backtracks on History to Settle Mystery of Explorer's Demise." *Washington Post* (30 May 1994): A3.

——. "Self Destruction on the Natchez Trace: Meriwether Lewis's Act of Ultimate Courage." *Columbia* 13, no. 2 (Summer 1999): 3–6.

——. "Trail's End for Meriwether Lewis: The Role of Syphilis." Paper presented to the American Academy of Forensic Sciences, New York City, 21 February 1997. http://www.cosmos-club.org/journals/1997/raven.html; *COSMOS* (1997): 1–6.

——. "Triumph Then Despair: The Tragic Death of Meriwether Lewis." *Epidemiology* 5, no. 3 (May 1994): 366–79.

——. "Underlying Cause of Death of Meriwether Lewis." Paper presented at the Medical History of the American West Conference, Museum of the Rockies, Bozeman, Mont., 24 October 2001.

Rogers, Ann. "The Gunshots at Grinder's Stand: Assumptions about Their Sequence Can Lead Investigators Astray." *We Proceeded On* 31, no. 4 (November 2005): 39–40.

Ronda, James P. *Lewis and Clark among the Indians*. Lincoln: University of Nebraska Press, 1984.

Saindon, Robert A. "The 'Unhappy Affair' on Two Medicine River." *We Proceeded On* 28, no. 3 (August 2002): 12–25.

Sanddal, Nels D. "The Mystery of Death: A Response to Westefeld and Less." *Suicide and Life-Threatening Behavior* 34, no. 3 (Fall 2004): 228–32.

Sassaman, Richard. "The Meriwether Lewis Murder Mystery: Three Perspectives." *American History* 54, no. 2 (April 2003): 46.

Schwalbe, David. "The Death of Meriwether Lewis." *American History* (22 November 1999).

"Senator Requests Exhumation of Meriwether Lewis." *Perspectives* (April 2002): 23.

Shuman, Malcolm. *The Meriwether Murder*. New York: Avon Books, 1998.

Southwick, Leslie H. "Peter Wagener Grayson." Handbook of Texas Online. http://www.tsha.utexas.edu/handbook/online/articles/view/GG/fgr29.html.

Starrs, James E. "The Death of a Hero: Meriwether Lewis—Suicide or Homicide?" *Scientific Sleuthing Review* 20, no. 2 (Summer 1996): 1–6.

——. *Meriwether Lewis, His Death and His Monument: An Historical and Pictorial Portfolio*. Washington, D.C.: James E. Starrs, 1997.

——. *A Voice for the Dead A Forensic Investigator's Pursuit of the Truth in the Grave*. With Katherine Ramsland. New York: Putnam, 2005.

Tennant, Brad. "Sexual Relations of the Lewis and Clark Expedition." In *The Lewis and Clark Expedition: Then and Now*, edited by David Kvernes. Sioux Falls, S.Dak.: Center for Western Studies, Augustana College, 2004.

Thompson, Harry F. "Meriwether Lewis and His Son: The Claim of Joseph DeSomet Lewis and the Problem of History." *North Dakota History* 67, no. 3 (2000): 24–37.

Thwaites, Reuben G., ed. *Original Journals of the Lewis and Clark Expedition, 1804–1806.* 8 vols. New York: Dodd, Mead, 1904–1905.

Townsend Genealogical Database. "Russell Family." http://www.Ancestry.com.

Tubbs, Stephenie Ambrose, and Clay S. Jenkinson. *The Lewis and Clark Companion: An Encyclopedia Guide to the Voyage of Discovery.* New York: Henry Holt, 2003.

Webster, William J. "Death of Gen. Lewis." *Nashville American,* 23 May 1904. Letter to editor.

Westefeld, John S. and Aaron Less. "Meriwether Lewis: Was it Suicide?" *Suicide and Life-Threatening Behavior* 34, no. 3 (Fall 2004): 220–27.

Wheeler, Olin D. *The Trail of Lewis and Clark, 1804–1904.* 2 vols. New York: G. P. Putnam's Sons, 1904.

White, Marian B. "A Great Explorer's Final Hours." *Frontier Times* (May 1980): 8–11, 45–50.

White, Robert H., ed. "Report of the Lewis Monument Committee, 31 January 1848." In *Messages of the Governors of Tennessee-1845–1857.* Vol. 4: 385–87. Nashville, Tenn.: Tennessee Historical Commission, 1952–1972.

Wilson, Alexander. "Particulars of the Death of Capt. Lewis." [In letter to Alexander Lawson.] *The Port Folio* (Philadelphia) 7, no. 1 (January 1812): 34–47.

Wilson, Charles M. *Meriwether Lewis of Lewis and Clark.* New York: Thomas Y. Crowell, 1934.

Woodhouse, Leighton. "Who Killed Meriwether Lewis?" Salon Ivory Tower. http://www.salon.com/it/feature/1999/03/22feature.html. Posted on 22 March 1999.

Zickler, Patrick. "A Lewis and Clark Post-Mortem–Homicide?: Lewis to Be Cleansed of the Taint of Suicide?" *Virginia* 19, no. 2 (1996): 26–29.

# Index